W9-AUY-435

Quilt-As-You-Go

Quilt-As-You-Go

Second Edition

Sandra Millett

Chilton Book Company | Radnor, Pennsylvania

Copyright © 1994, 1982 by Sandra Millett
Second Edition   All Rights Reserved
Published in Radnor, Pennsylvania 19089, by Chilton Book Company

No part of this book may be reproduced, transmitted or stored
in any form or by an means, electronic or mechanical,
without prior written permission from the publishers

All illustrations and photographs by the author
Designed by Rita Naughton for Spectrum Publisher Services
Manufactured in the United States of America

Library of Congress Cataloging in Publication Data

Millett, Sandra.
    Quilt-as-you-go / Sandra Millett. — 2nd ed.
        p.   cm.
    Includes bibliographical references and index.
    ISBN 0-8019-8357-6.
    1. Quilting. I. Title.
TT835.M53   1993
746.9'7—dc20
                                                    93-6384
                                                    CIP

1 2 3 4 5 6 7 8 9 0   3 2 1 0 9 8 7 6 5 4

This book is dedicated to the first quilters. In their desire for warmth, they have given us the gift of creation. With each patch and stitch, modern quilters are connected to history.

Contents

Acknowledgments

The Heritage Quilters have met once a week for twenty years. Though I don't live in the same state now, a telephone call to them brings instant help. Thanks to all of you for being my friends . . . and for the quilt samples.

To my husband, Derrill, who endures full clothes hampers—the flip side to empty dresser drawers—an overflowing kitchen sink, and few meals as a book deadline nears.

To PhotoCraft of Portland, Oregon. Your kindness and information have given me encouragement when I didn't have a clue about how to proceed. Thank you.

To Stephen Sipe, scanner extraordinaire, who learned more about quilt patterns than he ever wanted to know. That'll teach you to talk to a stranger in Powell's Books!

To the Romance Writers of America. While a member of four different chapters, I've learned writing techniques, found friends and generous colleagues, and improved my nonfiction writing. "Thank you" does not begin to express my gratitude.

Introduction

Quilts keep us warm, wrap our children in safe cocoons, decorate our homes, and are evidence to our descendants that we were creative, accomplished stitchers. Since the American Bicentennial in 1976, quilting has spread across our land and reached out to touch foreign shores. Japanese women have taken American quilting to their hearts, given it their own cultural flavor, and produced fabulous pieces. From Canada, England, and Germany, around the world to New Zealand and Australia, quilters have united by sharing ideas, techniques and enthusiasm.

In 1979, when two partners and I opened Quilters Paradise in Fresno, California, I remember fabric manufacturers' representatives saying that quilting would be around for ten years, the interest would fizzle out. Have quilters fooled them! In 1979 there were limited cotton colors and patterns available from the fabric mills. But today, anyone walking into a yardage store rejoices in the abundant selection of fabrics suitable for quilt-making.

As quilters conquered quiltmaking techniques, their horizons expanded to design, stretching the colorful bedcovering into art. Quilts now range from the expected to unusual shapes and surprising materials. The quilt has moved from beds onto walls, into museums, and into haute couture.

Nonquilters have frequently told me that I must have a lot of patience to make a quilt. My answer is an emphatic "No!" I am never patient, but I do persevere. Quilts are not made overnight, they require time, determination, and devotion. In return, they give beauty, color, a sense of accomplishment, and a record of needle proficiency.

Quilts are technical histories to quilters of their improving skills. Usually my students are not thrilled with their first attempts at applique. The first quarter of the block may not be what they want, but they see steady improvement as they work. They feel the same way about learning the punch-and-poke quilting stitch. After teaching quilting for almost twenty years, I've had only *six* students who could get straight stitches on the back of the quilt at the first try. I don't count myself among them!

This book is my eighteen-hour class in book form. It is structured for either an individual to use or as a teacher's textbook. A beginner can first master the basics, progress from easy to complex piecing and applique, and then go on to quilting and quilt assembly.

All readers (and my classroom students) are assumed to be beginners. There is a reason for this. When I began to teach myself quilting in 1975, I read books that taught how to piece and assemble a quilt, then said, "Quilt it." But I had a host of questions. What type of needle and thread? How long should I cut the thread? How do I hold the needle? How long should the stitches be? These were questions I finally answered for myself, after trial and error. Actually, a lot of error, and when I realized that other quilters had the same questions, I began teaching.

Each chapter adds additional techniques, building new skills on the just-learned. To be a quilter means more than doing the quilting stitch. First, you must learn to select compatible colors, choose a design, prepare the fabric, cut, piece, and join. Only then can you begin to quilt.

This new edition of *Quilt-As-You-Go* gives updated information, all new, original patterns, and an introduction to designing original quilts, in Chapter 13. It takes you from a tiny doodle to finished design, from fabric selection to finished wall hanging.

While the designing process varies from quiltmaker to quiltmaker, Chapter 13 gives a step-by-step method for designing that's easy to understand. It's the method I use when working out a new design. It also shows how a good design idea can go wrong when assembled in fabric, then how to salvage the piece.

Recently, I received a letter from a woman in Canada. She said, ". . . out of all the quilt books yours was the easiest to understand without bogging me down in what not to do's." It was signed, Dorothy Jeavons, Future Quilter.

To all future quilters like Dorothy, learn one step at a time and don't be discouraged by less than perfect results the first time or two. Quilting, like anything worthwhile, takes time, determination, love, and perserverance. Not necessarily patience.

Quilt-As-You-Go

Chapter One

Quilting Basics

If you are new at quilting, it's best to start by learning the basic vocabulary. Below are the words or phrases you will encounter in quilting. You'll find that there may be more than one term for the same definition. In that instance, I will generally use the older, more traditional one. I'll expand on some of the definitions when they are individually discussed in later chapters.

QUILTING TERMS

Quilt: A three-layer bed covering (top, batt, and backing) that is held together with a decorative pattern of short stitches going through all three layers. In simple language, it is a fabric sandwich!

Comforter: Similar to a quilt, with a top, batt, and backing. The top can be pieced, appliqued, or plain, as in a quilt, but it is not joined together with quilting stitches. It is held together with ties through all three layers, placed at regular intervals. Many people use the terms interchangeably, but to tie a unit does not begin to take the time it does to quilt it. Just ask a quilter about a comforter!

Top: The top layer of the quilt. The top may be pieced or appliqued, or it might simply be a large piece of fabric with a quilting design marked on it. In any case, it is the portion you want the world to see.

Batt: The soft middle layer of the quilt. The batt provides the quilt's warmth and fluffiness. Batts may be made from cotton, polyester (my choice), or wool.

Backing or lining: The back, or bottom layer, of the quilt. It can be a solid color or print fabric, and should be similar in weight to the top.

Quilting: The stitching together of the three quilt layers using short, even stitches. The stitches can follow the pattern of the patches or applique, or can follow an elaborate design marked on the top. To have a fine quality quilt, the stitches and the spaces between the stitches should be the same length on the top of the quilt as on the back. That's one of the things that make a quilt of heirloom quality and separate the truly superb quilters from the average!

Patchwork: Joining small pieces of fabric into a completed design. It can be either pieced or appliqued work.

Block: One finished unit of a quilt pattern. In this book the blocks are 16 inches square.

Piecing: Sewing small pieces of fabric together to form the block, i.e., you piece or applique patchwork.

1

Applique: Small pieces of fabric arranged in a pattern on a background block and sewn in place with a tiny blind stitch. The finished product is a design of layered fabric.

Setting blocks: Joining finished blocks to form a quilt top. The entire quilt top can be set together into strips for the quilt-as-you-go frame.

Sashing, strips, lattice: Narrow strips of fabric used to separate the blocks. Sashing only goes between blocks, never between a block and border. The sampler quilt must use sashing, because every block is a different pattern and each must be separated from its neighbor so that the individual patterns can be seen.

Border: The fabric strips that surround the completed interior of the quilt, as a frame surrounds a painting. You can use a single, double, or triple border, and multiple borders in some instances. The single border should always be the same color as the sashing. In the case of multiple borders, the inner border and sashing are the same color. This unifies the quilt and helps carry the eye throughout the quilt's design.

Binding: Binding is the narrow finished edge of the quilt. It is sewn over the outside edge of the border to cover the raw edges. It can be either a separate piece of fabric that is sewn on, or the backing fabric that has been brought over the edge of the border to the front and sewn down.

Strip, unit: A long section of blocks and sashing, if used, set together and ready to be basted to the batt and backing. The basted strip will go into the quilt-as-you-go frame for quilting.

Marking: Tracing the quilting design onto the quilt top. This can be done before the blocks have been set together and a strip is ready to be basted to the batt and backing. It can also be done after the quilt is in the frame.

Quilt-as-you-go: A method of assembling the quilt top in strips for quilting in a small lap frame. These quilted strips are then joined into a full-size quilt. This method eliminates the need for a large, 10-foot quilting frame and enables you to carry your quilting with you. This technique will be detailed in a later chapter. You do not quilt each block separately since assembly of individual blocks creates major problems.

Quilt patterns: The individual quilt block designs.

Quilting patterns or designs: Patterns for the short quilting stitches. These designs may be very elaborate or just simple straight lines.

Master pattern theory: A method of transferring both applique and quilting designs to the quilt top. This will be discussed in extensive detail in Chapter 7.

Sampler quilt: A quilt in which each block is a different pattern. Sampler quilts use sashing between the blocks so that each block stands alone.

Block-to-block assembly: Each block is the same pattern (usually) and is set together without sashing.

Alternate block assembly: One block is a pieced or appliqued pattern and the next block is plain fabric with a fancy quilting design. The rows are alternated.

SUPPLIES

Most new quilters will find they have many of the quilting supplies on hand. Remember, our early settlers had to make do with very little and usually had only the simplest equipment. If you don't have what I suggest, the key word is *improvise*.

Pencil

Use a soft #2 lead pencil and keep it very sharp! If you tire of constantly sharpening your pencil, buy one that uses separate pieces of lead of *fine* diameter and #B softness. These pencils can be found in stationery, art supply, or drafting stores. It is very important to keep in mind that only very light pressure can be used when marking on fabrics. If a line is too dark, it can never be removed. *Never* use a pen on fabric.

Pins

Use fine, sharp pins. I like the ones with glass heads because they are somewhat easier to grip. If you live near a florist, you might want to purchase a box of boutonniere pins. These have long shafts and large heads. In any case, throw away all the old, bent pins you've been using for the last ten years! Pins are meant to hold the fabric together, not punch holes in it.

Ruler

A short, metal dressmaker's ruler (hemming gauge) works well for making small templates and marking quilting lines. You'll also find that a yardstick will be useful for longer measurements. You might like to try the clear plastic ruler, 18 inches long and 2 inches wide, that is marked off in a grid pattern of ⅟₁₆-inch squares. This can be purchased at either art supply or drafting stores.

Needles

Sharps: These are the long, slender needles with a small eye that are used for all piecing and applique, setting of blocks, sewing strips together, and attaching the binding. In short, everything except the quilting will be done with a "sharp." Needles are sized so that the larger the number, the finer the needle. A #8 is larger than a #10, which is the finest "sharp" available for hand sewing. I prefer to use the #10, since it is very fine and glides through the material instead of punching holes. I urge all my students to use it at first, and most find they can handle it quite easily. This needle is so thin that, after a short period of time, it will bend to fit your fingers. This actually makes it easier to use. The only problem comes with threading the tiny eye. One solution is to thread a whole packet of needles onto the spool of thread. When you need more thread, pull it through the eyes of all the needles and leave the last needle on the length cut off. If this needle still presents a problem, try an embroidery needle. They come in the same sizes as "sharps," but the eyes are longer and therefore somewhat easier to thread. In any instance, don't use a needle larger than a #8 unless you have special vision problems.

Quilting or betweens: Quilting needles or betweens (same needle, two names) are used for all the actual quilting. They are short, fat needles with round eyes. I use a #9 needle, which is the finest needle generally available for quilting. If you find this size too difficult to thead, use a #8 or #7. Don't use anything larger than a #7, because it will leave holes in the fabric.

Batts

Polyester batts are made in three ways: bonded, unbonded, and felted or needled. Bonded batts can be bonded on the surface or all through the fibers. Felted batts are quite thin. Both types usually do not shift. Batting sold by the yard is stiff, uneven and really intended for upholstery. Cotton batts shift and need to be quilted every inch, as do unbonded polyester batts.

Thread

There are two types of thread to use. For all piecing and applique and assembly of the quilt, use #50 thread in a color that matches your fabric. This is used with the "sharp" needle. If you are using a variety of colors in the block, choose a thread color that seems to blend well with all the fabrics. You can use cotton-covered polyester or all-cotton thread. I prefer the 100% cotton, since it doesn't twist or get slipknots as readily. All-polyester thread tends to tangle very easily. I wax all my thread to prevent fraying and slipknots.

Quilting thread is so stiff that it should be used only for the actual quilting stitch, not for piecing or applique. It is heavier than #50 thread and is sometimes called "extra-strong" or "super-strength." Do not use buttonhole twist thread, as it is too heavy. Some brands are prewaxed (indicated on the spool). Quilting thread is used only with the quilting or "between" needle.

A white, lightweight thread called Brooks Basting Threads breaks very easily and is meant for temporary stitching or basting. It is much cheaper to use for basting your quilts together than regular mercerized thread.

Beeswax

This was once a common item in a sewing basket, but today only a few women know its purpose. A length of thread is cut from the spool and drawn across the edge or surface of the wax. The wax coats the thread and will greatly decrease the amount of twisting, slipknots, and fraying that occur with hand sewing. If you use polyester thread, you will especially notice the difference. Of course, this applies to all hand sewing, including dressmaking. Remember to remove the excess wax by pulling the thread between your fingers. Beeswax can be purchased in fabric stores or in hardware or sporting goods stores.

Paper

A white paper will be needed for master patterns. You can use white shelf paper, pattern drafting paper, artist's drawing paper, or sheets of typing paper that have been taped together.

Scissors

It doesn't matter what type you use as long as they are sharp! Keep a separate pair for cutting paper and templates. *Never* use fabric scissors to cut paper.

Template material

This is a sturdy material used to make the actual size patterns. The traditional method for making a template is to draw the pattern as accurately as possible on regular paper and then to cut it out without adding seam allowances. This paper pattern is then glued to the smooth (paper) side of fine sandpaper. (The sandpaper will prevent the template from slipping as you trace around it.) When the glue is dry, the excess sandpaper is cut off at the edge of the pattern. The template is now ready to use. It should be positioned on the wrong side of the fabric (sandpaper side to the fabric) and traced with a pencil. Your pencil line now duplicates the template. Cut the patch from the fabric, adding a ¼-inch seam allowance as you cut.

Many quilters still use the above method, but there are two drawbacks with sandpaper. First, you can't see through the sandpaper, so if you want to center a design, you have to guess at the placement. The second problem is that the edges wear down as you repeatedly trace around them. This makes it impossible to obtain the accuracy necessary when using a pattern like Miner's Lamp where ¹⁄₃₂ of an inch can throw off your entire design. The only solution is to replace each template as it begins to wear down. Thus, if you have to cut 3000 hexagons for the quilt top, you'll need to make at least 40 or 50 master templates before you can even put one line on the fabric. That's a lot of extra work!

One way to eliminate these problems is to use a thin, clear, rigid plastic which won't wear away on the edges and has the advantage of transparency for placement of fabric designs. There are several types of plastic that can be used. If you have access to a drafting or art supply store, you can buy acetate Mylar in several thicknesses. I prefer .0075-mil, but either .010- or .005-mil work well also. Be sure to get the type that has a matte or frosty finish on one side. If the Mylar is smooth on both sides you won't be able to write on it. For those quilters who are not able to find Mylar there are several other options. Bacon often comes packaged on plastic sheets that work very nicely and usually have one rough side that can be written on. Some of my students have used old

plastic bottles. These are usually not clear and tend to be fairly thick, so care must be used in cutting. Old X-ray film is another source for template material. You can ask hospitals and X-ray labs to save it for you. Rough up one side with fine sandpaper so you'll be able to write on it. Regardless of what template material you use, do not cut it with good fabric scissors; use a pair you don't care about.

Iron

Steam irons work very nicely, but I prefer a plain dry iron used in conjunction with a spray bottle of water. The iron is light and its tip is smaller and more pointed than that of a steam iron. Also, my steam iron always burps out big, brown stains just as I place it on the fabric (see Chapter 5: Pressing).

MAKING A QUILT-AS-YOU-GO FRAME

The quilt-as-you-go frame is very easy to make. You'll need a hammer, drill, saw, and about forty minutes of time. The dowel lengths can be made to fit widths of up to 30 inches or more. All frames will hold a 100-inch strip. For general use, a 24-inch frame (a 48-inch dowel cut in half) is best. I have frames ranging in size from 12 inches to 36 inches, but the latter is really much too long to handle comfortably.

Supplies Needed

1. 24 inches of 1″ × 2″ clear pine or fir. You really can use any type of wood, but if a dense wood such as oak is used, the frame will get a bit heavy to handle.

2. 48 inches of ¾″ dowel or any length desired.

3. 4 hanger bolts. These are double-threaded, headless screws (Fig. 1–1). They can be purchased separately or in packages that contain swag lamp hooks.

4. 4 #10–24 wing nuts (³⁄₁₆″).

5. 4 #10 flat washers (³⁄₁₆″).

6. 48 inches of 1″-wide canvas tape. The tape has to be light enough to pin into, but not so flimsy that it will stretch. If you can't find it, use pillow ticking or heavy ribbon, such as grosgrain.

7. ⁴⁄₁₆″ upholstery tacks or a staple gun that uses a ¼″ staple leg.

8. Epoxy glue or a good white glue.

unthreaded section

Fig. 1-1 Use a hanger bolt (shown actual size) for inserting into the drilled dowel holes. They are also called double-threaded screws.

Assembly

1. Cut the 1″ × 2″ pine into two 12″ lengths and sand all the sides smooth.

2. Drill a hole in each end of the 12″ lengths. These holes are to be centered 1″ from each end of the boards. Drill the holes *larger* than the diameter of the hanger bolts. (The bolts should be able to slip through easily.) I use a ⁷⁄₃₂″ drill bit (Fig. 1–2a).

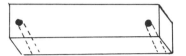

Fig. 1–2a Drill a hole into each end of the crossbar.

3. Cut the doweling into two 24″ lengths or any length desired. Drill a hole 1″ deep into both ends of each length of doweling (Fig. 1–2b). Use a ³⁄₁₆″ drill bit for this. Be sure that the holes are drilled straight, or the bolts will be at an angle when set in. It helps to have a vise to hold the dowel while you do the drilling.

Fig. 1–2b Drill centered holes into each end of the dowel.

4. Tack the canvas tape (or whatever you're using) down the length of the doweling, making sure that the tape is in a straight line. Turn ½″ of the tape under on each end. Start and end the tape ½″ in from the ends of the doweling so that you will have a 23″ finished length of tape on the 24″ dowel (Fig. 1–2c). If you live in an area of high humidity, coat the tacks or staples with clear nail polish to prevent rust stains on your fabric.

Fig. 1–2c Attach canvas tape to each dowel, using either upholstery tacks or a staple gun.

5. Roll the pointed end of the hanger bolt in the prepared glue so that the threads are well covered. Push the bolts into the holes in the ends of the dowel.

You may have to tap the bolts lightly with a hammer to coax them in. Be sure you leave the top, threaded area of the bolt sticking out far enough so that you can put the 12″ end piece over the bolt and still be able to put on a washer and wing nut (Fig. 1–2d). Let the glue dry thoroughly.

Fig. 1–2d Roll the long end of the hanger bolt in glue and then tap it into the dowel hole with a hammer.

6. Now put the projecting bolts into the end pieces and place a washer and wing nut over the metal portion sticking out of the holes. Notice that in the diagram the dowels have been inserted so that the loose edges of the tape face each other (Fig. 1–2e) and the tacks or staples are on top of the dowels. The arrows indicate which way the dowels are to be rotated after the strip is pinned or based into the frame.

Fig. 1–2e Insert the projecting bolts into the drilled holes in the end bars.

STEPS IN MAKING A QUILT

When learning any new technique, it's easy to get bogged down in the "how to's" and forget the proper sequence of events. For that reason, I have listed the steps in making a quilt.

1. Choose the pattern.

2. Choose the fabric. These first two steps can be reversed. You might have fabric on hand and look for a block pattern that will enhance it. Or you may fall

in love with a particular pattern and then shop for complementary fabrics.

3. Wash and iron all the fabric. Use hot water to be sure that it has shrunk and bled all it's going to. If you're using muslin, wash and dry it at least twice, as it shrinks more than once. The only things you don't wash are the batt and thread.

4. Check your template for accuracy. This is explained in detail in Chapter 3.

5. Cut out the template (see Chapter 3).

6. Use a sharp #2 lead pencil to trace around the template that has been placed on the wrong side of the material (see Chapter 3).

7. Piece or applique the blocks. You must iron as you go when you are piecing. If you are appliqueing, no ironing is necessary, except for the background block. As a general rule, if you piece your entire block and then press it when it's completed, it won't look as crisp as it will if you press each of the small sections as they are completed.

8. Set the blocks together in strips (see Chapter 9).

9. Mark the quilting patterns on the top. For sashing or borders you may choose to do the marking before setting it together (see Chapter 9).

10. Baste the top strip, batt, and backing together (see Chapter 9).

11. Set the strip into the quilt-as-you-go frame (see Chapter 10).

12. Quilt the strip (see Chapter 10).

13. Repeat Steps 6 through 12 to make as many strips as necessary for the entire quilt, including the borders. The borders are usually not set to the blocks, but treated as separate strips.

14. Join the strips together to form the interior of the quilt. The quilted border strips are then added to the outer edges of the quilt interior.

15. Bind the edges (see Chapter 11).

16. Enjoy!

One of the terrific things about the quilt-as-you-go method is that once you have two strips made, they can be joined together and you can really see what you are accomplishing. I usually put two strips together and place them across my bed to see how they look. You can even lie down under a long strip to try it out. You may not be covered too completely, but you'll sure look great!

Chapter Two

Fabrics: Colors, Kinds, Combinations

CHOOSING FABRICS

The most important concern of all quilters is what type of fabric to use. Cotton or cotton blend fabrics are generally used for traditional quilts as they are the easiest to work with, especially for a beginner. Also, it has been proven that cotton quilts stand the test of time best. If you can't find 100 percent cotton, use a cotton blend fabric, but try to avoid 65 percent polyester, 35 percent cotton if you are new to quilting. These blends usually fray badly, and a beginner will find it very difficult to handle the small patches. Also, if you are new to my method, where no basting or pressing is done while appliqueing, don't use a high percent blend. If the fabric frays badly or is silky, as is frequently the case with 65/35 blends, you are going to have more problems than necessary.

Try to choose fabrics that have a good, tight weave. If you are a beginner, try to use as much 100 percent cotton or 50/50 blend as possible. If you can't find the color or print you need in these blends, you'll have no choice but to use a 65/35 fabric. A number of quilters are hesitant to use cotton because of its tendency to wrinkle and bleed. Remember, cotton fabrics today are not what they were twenty or thirty years ago. Many are permanent press and need little or no ironing. The modern fabrics don't usually bleed color as they used to either, but always wash your fabric to shrink it and to remove any excess dye and finish.

It doesn't matter if you use scraps on hand or buy all new fabric, as long as the materials are all similar in weight and fiber content. Do not use seersucker (too puckery), sheer fabrics, laces, or single or double knits. While knits work well for simple shapes, i.e., squares, triangles, and rectangles that are machine pieced, they are usually too thick for involved hand piecing or applique, and they make very heavy seams. However, if you want to try them, I wish you luck!

If you do have scraps you want to use, you're

ahead of the game. In that case, you will probably need to purchase only the fabric for sashing, borders, and backing. If you don't have scraps, all the fabric will have to be purchased. In either case, the colors should be coordinated to tie the quilt together visually (see color Fig. 1).

CHOOSING COLORS

Probably the biggest problem for new quilters is choosing colors. After selecting material for a few quilts, you'll find it will be one of the most exciting tasks in making a quilt. At first you may feel completely lost, but there are some guides to follow and it really does get easier.

The best single item to help you is a color wheel, commonly used by artists and decorators. It is a circle that is divided equally into 12 solid color wedges, starting with yellow at the top and moving in color succession as a rainbow. Although we quilters work with fabrics that can have many colors in their designs, usually a fabric has a dominant color (it may

not be the background color), and that would be the color on the wheel. It would help a great deal for you to make a color wheel from patterned fabrics, as shown in color Figure 9. Take it with you when shopping to help in selecting colors. I have provided a color wheel template so that you can make your own (Fig. 2–1).

Using a color wheel is not difficult. There are a number of methods in working from the wheel. Select from one of the groupings listed below, stick to it, and your quilt will be very eye-catching.

Triad: Three colors that are an equal distance apart on the wheel; in other words, every fourth color. Let's suppose you want to use orange. Green and purple are the triads. You may not care for the strong, pure colors, but what if you use the softer tones of peach, pale green and lavender? Yellow, blue, and red softened with white are pale yellow, baby blue, and pink. Now you know why those three colors look so good in a baby's room; it's a triad. You could also use one strong color, blue-violet (blueberry), light grass green (lime), and soft red-orange (light rust).

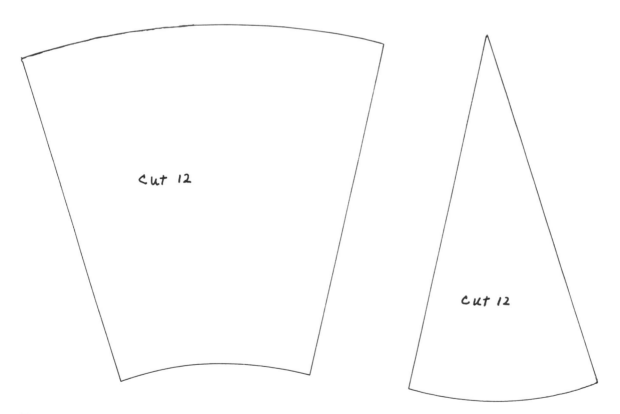

Cut 12

Cut 12

Fig. 2-1 The color wheel template (also see color Fig. 9). Cut twelve of each patch. Piece the wheel following the directions in Chapter 8.

Complementary: Opposite colors on the wheel complement each other. Green and red (Christmas) or purple and yellow are examples.

Analogous: Colors that are next to each other on the color wheel. The cool colors are the greens, blues and purples. The warm colors are reds, oranges and yellows.

Polychromatic: This is a color scheme using all of the colors from around the color wheel: yellow, green, blue, purple, red, and orange.

Achromatic: These are the neutral colors: white, black, brown, beige, and gray. These colors are not found on the color wheel, because they are really "noncolors."

Monochromatic: A one-color scheme. For example, the palest pink, bright pink, red, and deep, ruby red.

COMBINING PRINTS

Harmonious (pleasing) colors play a very important part in the overall effect of your quilt; but equally important is the mixture of solid colors and prints. Strong solid colors in a geometric pattern will look very contemporary. A mixture of small prints in faded colors will have an old, very traditional feel. The combination of solids, prints and colors are endless, and selecting them offers you a challenging job, for you will want your quilt to suit the location you have chosen for it.

For years, while growing up, you were told that you couldn't wear two prints at the same time and, if you tried three, Heaven forbid, the world would surely end! As a quilter you must forget those early lessons. Two or more prints do go together, and more often than not, they add more interest than just a variety of solid colors and one print.

The burning question is, how do you choose not only the right colors, but compatible prints? I pick one fabric I like, either a print or solid, then try different color and print combinations until I'm satisfied. Sometimes, by the time I make my final selection, I have eliminated the original fabric choice. Remember, be flexible! Don't feel you must use a fabric just because you happen to have it. You'll eventually find the right spot for it in another quilt.

It can take from ten minutes in one store, to days in many stores, to find that final "perfect" piece of fabric. When I was a partner in a quilt shop, I had one customer who came in two days in a row and spent four hours each day selecting fabric for a quilt. I was numb by then, and she had wasted seven hours. Sometimes your first instincts are the best. Too much pondering leads to confusion!

My formula for mixing prints pleasingly was acquired while helping many customers select the right combinations. I found that when working in conjunction with the color wheel, you can effectively mix

Fig. 2-2 Examples of the print mixing formula. In a black-and-white photo the designs and background variations become very pronounced.

fabrics with the following design combinations: (Fig. 2–2)

   1. A print with lots of background color showing, and little pattern design;

   2. An even mixture of background color and pattern design;

   3. Heavy pattern design, with little background color showing.

   If you use this print formula, along with the color wheel, you'll find fabric selection much easier and really a lot of fun.

PREPARING THE FABRIC

Some fabrics will shrink more than others. You need to eliminate all shrinkage before you start piecing. Wash all fabrics in hot water and dry them on your dryer's "hot" setting. Wash and dry muslin twice. After the fabric is washed, iron it, if necessary. *Do not* wash the batt or thread.

Chapter Three

Patterns and Templates

CHECKING PATTERN ACCURACY

While you are preparing the fabric, the templates can be made. How do you know if the block pattern a friend has given you, or that you found in a book, is accurate? You don't; therefore, you *must* assume that it is inaccurate. I know that this is a blow to most of you, especially those of you who have a large library of quilting books. If your pieced blocks haven't been lying flat when completed, this is the reason. Of all the books I own, there are only two or maybe three with which I feel safe working directly from the patterns without checking for accuracy. I don't let this stop me from purchasing books, however. I use them as resource material and as a starting point for drafting.

Certainly your next question must be, "Why the inaccuracy?" There are several reasons. A number of the old books are reprints from newspapers, and the distortion from the printing presses has been magnified over the years. In the newer books, again some distortion has occurred because of the printing, but it can't all be blamed on the reproduction process. Some authors and publishing houses do not realize how critical accuracy in quilt patterns is.

I think most of us believe that all "old time" quilts

were perfect. If you take a really close look (or many times just a glance), you'll find that this is not the case. There were women then, as now, who didn't enjoy quilting, but had no choice in the matter. Bed coverings had to be made! Of the thousands of quilts that have been made, worn out and discarded, many were just "thrown together." When I see a quilt like that, I feel a particular kinship with the maker. One hundred years ago that women had to do things she wasn't very crazy about either, but she had no alternatives.

How can you tell if your pattern is accurate? First, simply look at it. Some patterns are so far off you can see that template A is too long to fit to template B. The next step is to measure each of the template edges. If it's a square, all the sides should be the same length and have right-angle corners (90 degrees). Check each of the patch patterns with a ruler to see if the edges that will be sewn together are the same length. If not, then something is going to have to be done about it. Sometimes it's as simple as moving one line just a bit, but more often than not, it means that you will have to work with graph paper and a ruler. Please, don't let that scare you away; it is not as hard as you might think. Drafting patterns is covered in detail in Chapter 12.

MAKING TEMPLATES

After making sure that your pattern is accurate, you must make a template for each of the patches. It is extremely important that all marking and cutting be done carefully.

Note: For hand piecing, seam allowances *should not* be added to the template patterns. They will be allowed for when cutting. If you are making templates for machine piecing, then you *must* add a ¼-inch seam allowance to the template.

Place the template material (assuming you are using clear, Mylar acetate) over the accurate paper pattern. Using a rule as a guide, trace over the pattern line to duplicate the pattern on the plastic. Be sure that you have made an exact copy, paying special attention to the corners. Use an old, but sharp, pair of scissors to cut out the template. Be accurate in cutting, and make sure the points are nice and sharp with straight edges. Now lay the plastic template back over the original pattern to check it for accuracy. If the template doesn't match the pattern, don't use it; make a better one. Be sure not to cut out the original paper pattern as a template. Keep it as a permanent reference.

If you are not using plastic, then use a piece of typing or writing paper and position it over the accurate pattern. With a ruler as a guide, copy the template pattern onto the typing paper. If you have trouble seeing the lines of the pattern through the typing paper, tape both pieces of paper to a window and the lines will be visible. Cut out the template copy and glue it to a firm piece of opaque plastic (coffee can lid) or stiff paper, such as a manila folder. The paper side of fine sandpaper can also be used. Let the glue dry and then cut the excess stiff template material away. Do remember, if you use a cardboard or sandpaper template, it will wear down after repeated use and, you'll need to make others (see Chapter 1).

I have mentioned accuracy quite a few times. I know that at this point it probably sounds picky to you to make such a fuss about it, but a little extra care now will save you much agony later on. I have seen finished blocks, for the same quilt, that varied as much as three inches in size; a Lone Star that rippled like a wave and would never lie flat; a Broken Star so large it flowed twelve inches onto the floor.

POSITIONING TEMPLATES

You are almost ready to mark and cut the fabric, but you must be aware of fabric straight-of-grain before placing your template on the material.

Cotton fabric is made by first stringing threads lengthwise on a loom; then another thread is interwoven through each of the lengthwise threads. The threads running the length of the fabric are called the "warp" and the threads interweaving them are the "woof." The woven edge of the fabric is called the "selvage." The selvages frequently shrink a great deal when washed and, thus, should be cut off and discarded. The actual straight-of-grain is the warp, but for a quilter both the warp and woof can be consid-

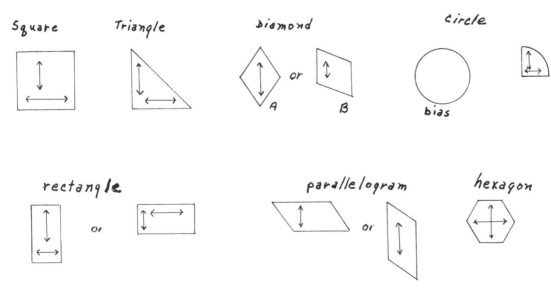

Fig. 3-1 The arrows indicate the directions in which to place the geometric shapes on fabric straight-of-grain.

ered the straight. If you pull on the diagonal, there will be a great deal of give. This is the "bias." A true bias is on a 45-degree angle to the selvage.

When you trace the template on the fabric, you should have as many straight edges of the template on the straight-of-grain as possible. The diagrams have arrows indicating the direction in which the templates should be placed on the fabric (Fig. 3–1). Both the warp and woof are given for the square and triangle. I have given two choices for the diamond. In diamond A, the straight is placed down the center length of the diamond and all the edges are on the bias. Cutting diamond B places two edges on the straight and two on the bias. Diamonds are frequently used to make stars where the most tension would be from point to point; therefore diamond A would be used most often. The same applies to the parallelogram, in that two placements are possible. The hexagon can have only two edges on the grain because of its shape. A circle, of course, has no straight sides, so all the edges are on the bias.

Now that I've given you some rules to follow, I'm going to contradict myself and say that you can disregard them if you want to. If there is a pattern or stripe in the fabric that you want to take advantage of, the template can be placed accordingly. This will frequently be the case with odd-shaped applique patches, where most of the edges are on the bias. If possible, try to have the straight running the longest span of the template. You must be very careful in sewing and pressing these patches, since all bias edges will stretch very easily.

MARKING THE FABRIC

Your fabric should now be prepared: washed, dried, and ironed. Lay it on a table, wrong side up. Place the template, matte or sandpaper side down, on the fabric following the straight-of-grain or fabric design and close enough to the edge to leave a 1/4-inch seam allowance around it if you are hand piecing.

Using a very sharp #2 pencil (no pens, please), mark around the edge of the template so that the template outline is duplicated on the fabric with a fine, light line. The fabric will tend to shift and pull, especially at the template corners. If you hold the pencil at an angle and draw it across the fabric, the pulling is not quite as bad. Working with a sharp pencil and lifting it occasionally to let the fabric return to its normal position helps too. Press down just hard enough to mark the fabric; you don't need a heavy, dark line. Try to train yourself to draw only a

single line. Avoid scratching around the template. A single, fine line will do (see Fig. 6–7).

On some print or dark fabrics, pencil lines won't show. For these materials use a sliver of white soap for the marking instead of a pencil. After your hand soap has been used down to a small piece, let it dry on a windowsill for a few days; the edge will make a good marker. Don't use colored soap, since the dye might leave a stain on the fabric. The soap-marked patches need to be handled carefully, since the soap lines will rub off. A tailor's chalk pencil can be used instead, but I have found that they don't sharpen well. Also you have to apply a lot of pressure to make a line. There is a water soluble pen available today that is terrific; however, some types tend to vanish in a few days or may not wash out. Test on a scrap before using.

CUTTING AND STORING THE PATCHES

For hand piecing, the template lines have been drawn on the fabric so that there is a 1/4-inch space around each shape. In other words, there is 1/2-inch between each of the shapes. Using sharp scissors, cut down the middle of the space between the patches; this will automatically leave a 1/4-inch seam allowance on each patch (Fig. 3–2).

In this book I deal only with hand work, both for piecing and quilting, but the techniques are basically the same for machine work. When machine piecing, the templates have the seam allowances included, so the pencil lines become the cutting lines. With most sewing machines, the distance from the outer edge of

Fig. 3-2 Various templates for hand piecing traced onto the wrong side of the fabric. A 1/2-inch space is left between each shape to allow for seam allowances. The cutting lines are indicated by broken lines.

Fig. 3-3 String all the patches of one shape onto a knotted thread.

the presser foot to the needle is ¼ inch. Check your machine to see if there is a variation and then make the necessary adjustments when sewing. The patches are fed into the machine with the cut edges lined up with the presser foot edge. The stitching line will automatically leave a ¼-inch seam allowance.

After the patches have been cut they tend to get lost if not contained in some way. Boxes filled with neat stacks of patches are always being knocked over, and then confusion reigns. It's a good idea to string each pile of matching patches onto a knotted, white thread (Fig. 3–3). The knot is placed at the bottom of the stack and a patch is pulled off the loose thread as needed. It's difficult to tell some patches apart, so make a label from scrap fabric and mark it with the patch designation. String the label onto the knotted thread first, so it will be on the bottom of the stack.

Chapter Four

Sample Layouts and Cutting Methods

DETERMINING QUILT SIZE

How do you determine the quantity of fabric for a quilt project? Basically, a double-size quilt top with a 12-inch drop uses 6 yards and a king to the floor uses 12 to 17 yards, depending on the size of the patches. More and smaller patches mean many more seam allowances, and those ¼-inch allowances really gobble up the yardage.

Let's assume you want to make a double-bed quilt in three colors. If the three colors are going to be used in equal amounts, divide the 6 yards needed by the three colors. You'll need 2 yards of each color. I would buy 2½ yards of each to allow for shrinkage and mistakes.

Because this book deals with a sampler quilt, made to specific sizes, yardages have to be more than a "guesstimate." First, determine what size quilt is needed. Only then can you figure the yardage amounts accurately. (See Chapter 12 for detailed in-structions on figuring yardage.) If you are trying to fit a particular bed, you must measure it to determine how large the quilt needs to be. Start with the mattress dimensions below.

Mattress Top Measurements (in inches):

Crib	28 × 52
Twin	38 × 75
Double	54 × 75
Queen	60 × 75
King	72 × 85
Waterbed	72 × 104 to 108

There are many additional factors that must be taken into account in determining quilt size. Do you want the quilt to be used with a skirt? Mattress thickness varies from foam at 5 inches to innerspring ranging from 5 to 7 inches. If the quilt is to hang to the floor, is your bed on regular legs or casters? Large casters add 2 inches to the distance from mattress edge to floor. If you want the quilt to just touch the floor, as a bedspread would, that's important. How thick are the pillows? Big, fat ones need more quilt to cover them. If you intend to tuck the quilt under the pillows, it will add another 4 to 5 inches to the length. Maybe none of the above seems important to you; all you want to do is just make a quilt! That's fine too. Pick out the size that you want and get to work. But if you are going to make a quilt for a specific bed, then overall finished measurements are vital.

The actual quilting stitch draws up the quilt and reduces the finished size. Depending on how elaborate your quilting pattern is, you may have to add an extra 2 inches to both the length and width. These 2 inches should go into the borders, where your final size adjustments will be made. One of the advantages of quilt-as-you-go is that you can finish the entire interior of the quilt and lay it on the bed for a "fitting." Then you can tell if you need more or less width in the borders and, when finished, the quilt edge will be exactly where you want it.

The normal drop for a quilt used with a skirt is the mattress measurement plus 12 inches for each of the sides and bottom and 9 to 12 inches for a pillow allowance. For a quilt that drops to the floor, you would add 18 to 21 inches. For example, a double-bed mattress measures 54 by 75 inches. To make a quilt that will be used with a skirt, add 12 inches for each side to the 54-inch mattress width to get 78 inches. The 75-inch length is added to a 12-inch drop for the foot and a 9-inch fold-over for the pillow, for a total of 96 inches. Your quilt will measure 78 by 96 inches.

Below, I list some basic sizes for quilts intended to be used with a skirt or to extend to the floor. These are average sizes; your own needs may vary with your bed measurements.

YARDAGE REQUIREMENTS

Sampler quilts must have sashing or alternate blocks to separate the different block patterns. In Figures 4–1 through 4–20 you are given ten quilt layouts with yardage amounts for sashing or alternate blocks, borders, backing, and binding. Notice that some of the layouts have a single border, others double or triple. Multiple borders are used so that the need to piece additional blocks is reduced as much as possible. This is a book on how to handle different assembly problems, not necessarily a pattern book. Choose the quilt that fits your needs most closely, or make your own layout (see Chapter 12).

Exact yardage requirements for piecing and applique are not included. Because I don't know which blocks you will choose to make or how many colors you will use, it is impossible for me to do this. Assume the block is red, white, and blue. If blue is the predominant color with a little red and white, obviously more blue fabric will be needed. Therefore, you must determine which blocks you will make, how many colors you will use, and where they will be placed in order to accurately judge fabric needs. As a general rule, however, you can buy for each block: ¼ to ⅓ yard of each color, if three fabrics are used; ⅛ to ¼ yard of each color, if four fabrics are used. Then multiply the above amount by the number of total blocks to be made to get the yardage required. You will need ½ yard of 45-inch material for two 16-inch background blocks.

Finished Quilt Sizes (in inches):

Bed Type	With Skirt (12-inch drop)	To the Floor
Throw or Crib	44 × 64	—
Twin	62 × 96	78 × 104
Double	78 × 96	94 × 104
Queen	84 × 96	100 × 104
King	96 × 106	112 × 114
King Waterbed	80 × 117 (4-inch tuck)	

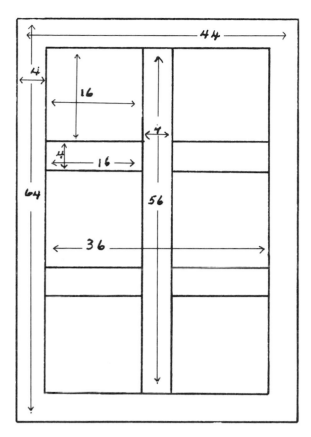

Fig. 4-1 Throw or crib quilt layout.

Fig. 4-2 Throw or crib quilt cutting methods. Finished size, 44″ × 64″; arrangement, 2 × 3 blocks, single border; block size, 16 inches square; sashing, 4 inches wide; borders, 4 inches wide; binding, ½ inch wide. Yardage required: sashing and borders, 1¼ yards; backing, 2¼ yards; binding, ⅜ yard.

Fig. 4-3 Twin with skirt layout.

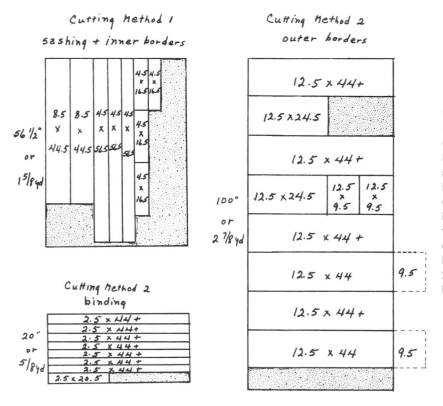

Fig. 4-4 Twin with skirt cutting methods. Finished size, 68" × 96"; arrangement, 2 × 3 blocks, double border; block size, 16 inches square; sashing, 4 inches wide; inner border, 4 inches wide (sides), 8 inches wide (top and bottom); outer border, 12 inches wide; binding, ½ inch wide. Yardage required: sashing and inner border, 1⅝ yards; outer borders, 2⅞ yards; backing, 5½ yards; binding, ⅝ yard.

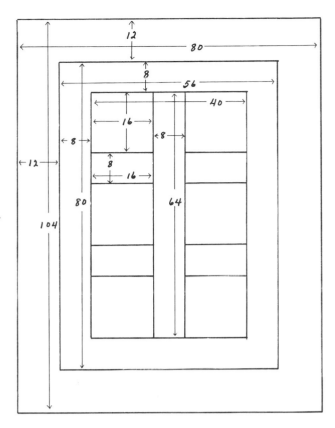

Fig. 4-5 Twin to floor layout.

Fig. 4-6 Twin to floor cutting methods. Finished size, 80" × 104"; arrangement, 2 × 3 blocks, double borders; block size, 16 inches square; sashing, 8 inches wide; inner borders, 8 inches wide; outer borders, 12 inches wide; binding, ½ inch wide. Yardage required: sashing and inner borders, 2½ yards; outer borders; 3¼ yards; backing, 5½ yards; binding, ⅝ yard.

Cutting Method 1
Sashing + inner border

Cutting Method 2
outer border

Cutting Method 2
binding

Fig. 4-7 Double with skirt layout.

Cutting Method 1

Cutting Method 2

Fig. 4-8 Double with skirt cutting methods. Finished size, 78″ × 98″; arrangement, 3 × 4 blocks, single border; block size, 16 inches square; sashing, 4 inches wide; borders, 11 inches wide; binding, ½ inch wide. Yardage required: Sashing and borders, 3⅞ yards; backing, 6 yards; binding, ⅞ yard.

Fig. 4-9 Double to floor layout.

Fig. 4-10 Double to floor cutting methods. Finished size, 98" × 98"; arrangement, 3 × 3 blocks, triple borders; block size, 16 inches square; sashing, 5 inches wide; inner borders, 5 inches wide; middle borders, 10 inches wide; outer borders, 5 inches wide; binding, ½ inch wide. Yardage required: sashing and inner borders, 2⅛ yards; middle borders, 2⅝ yards; outer borders, 1½ yards; backing, 7½ yards; binding, ¾ yard.

21

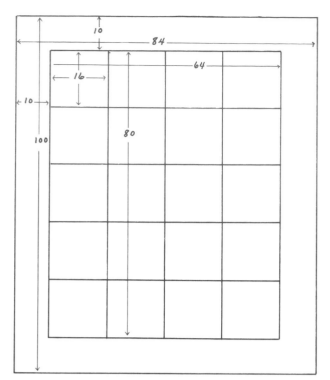

Fig. 4-11 Queen with skirt layout.

two possible alternate block arrangements

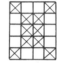

Cutting Method 1
alternate blocks

16.5 x 16.5	16.5 x 16.5
16.5 x 16.5	16.5 x 16.5
16.5 x 16.5	16.5 x 16.5
16.5 x 16.5	16.5 x 16.5
16.5 x 16.5	16.5 x 16.5

82½"
or
2⅜ yd

Cutting Method 2
border

94½"
or
2¾ yd

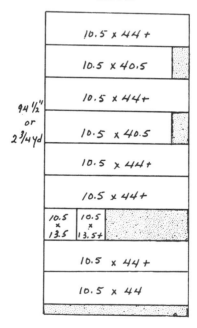

10.5 x 44+
10.5 x 40.5
10.5 x 44+
10.5 x 40.5
10.5 x 44+
10.5 x 44+
10.5 x 13.5   10.5 x 13.5+
10.5 x 44+
10.5 x 44

Cutting Method 2
binding

22½"
or
7/8 yd

2.5 x 44+
2.5 x 44+
2.5 x 44+
2.5 x 44+
2.5 x 44+
2.5 x 44+
2.5 x 44+
2.5 x 44+
2.5 x 22.5

Fig. 4-12 Queen with skirt cutting methods. Finished size, 84" × 100"; arrangement, 4 × 5 alternate blocks, single border; block size, 16 inches square; borders, 10 inches wide; binding, ½ inch wide. Yardage required: alternate blocks, 2⅜ yards; borders, 2¾ yards; backing, 7⅜ yards; binding, ⅞ yard.

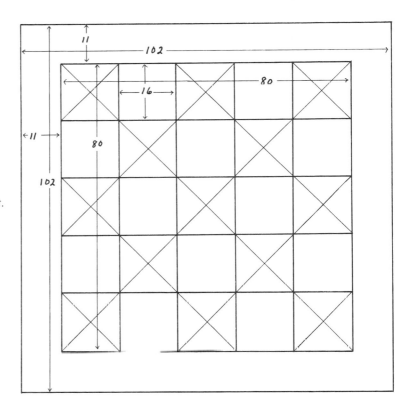

Fig. 4-13 Queen to floor layout.

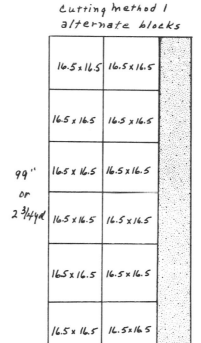

Fig. 4-14 Queen to floor cutting methods. Finished size, 102" × 102"; arrangement, 5 × 5 alternate blocks, single border; block size, 16 inches square; borders, 11 Inches wide; binding, ½ inch wide. Yardage required: alternate blocks, 2¾ yards; borders, 3¼ yards; backing, 7½ yards; binding, ⅞ yard.

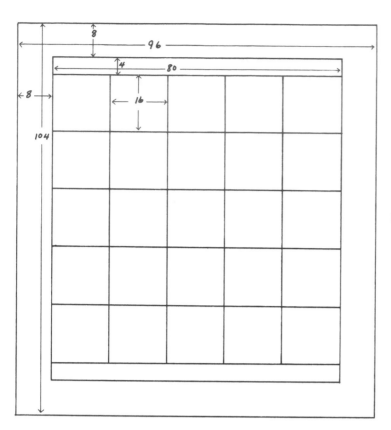

Fig. 4-15 King with skirt layout.

Cutting Method 1
alternate blocks

99"
or
2 3/4 yd

16.5 x 16.5	16.5 x 16.5
16.5 x 16.5	16.5 x 16.5
16.5 x 16.5	16.5 x 16.5
16.5 x 16.5	16.5 x 16.5
16.5 x 16.5	16.5 x 16.5
16.5 x 16.5	16.5 x 16.5

Cutting Method 2
outer border

85"
or
2 3/8 yd

8.5 x 44 +
8.5 x 44 +
8.5 x 17.5   8.5 x 26.5 +
8.5 x 44 +
8.5 x 35
8.5 x 44 +
8.5 x 44 +
8.5 x 9.5   8.5 x 9.5 +
8.5 x 44 +
8.5 x 44

Cutting Method 2
inset borders

18"
or
1/2 yd

4.5 x 44 +
4.5 x 37
4.5 x 44 +
4.5 x 37

Fig. 4-16 King with skirt cutting methods. Finished size, 96" × 104"; arrangement, 5 × 5 block to block, single border; block size, 16 inches square; inset borders, 4 inches wide (top and bottom); outer borders, 8 inches wide. Yardage required: alternate blocks (if desired), 2¾ yards; inset borders, ½ yard; outer borders, 2⅜ yards; backing, 7½ yards; binding, ¾ yard.

Cutting Method 2
binding

25"
or
3/4 yd

2.5 x 44 +
2.5 x 44 +
2.5 x 44 +
2.5 x 44 +
2.5 x 44 +
2.5 x 44 +
2.5 x 44 +
2.5 x 44 +
2.5 x 9.5

24

Fig. 4-17 King to floor layout.

Fig. 4-18 King to floor cutting methods. Finished size, 114″ × 114″; arrangement, 5 × 5 blocks, single border; block size, 16 inches square; sashing, 4 inches wide; borders, 9 inches wide; binding, ½ inch wide. Yardage required: sashing, 2¾ yards; borders, 3 yards; backing, 11 yards; binding, ⅞ yard.

Fig. 4-19 King waterbed layout.

Curring Method 1
sashing + inset border

Curring Method 2
outer border

Curring Method 2
binding

Fig. 4-20 King waterbed cutting methods. Finished size, 80" × 117"; arrangement, 3 × 4 blocks, single border; block size, 16 inches square; sashing, 5 inches wide; inset borders, 8 inches wide (top and bottom); outer borders, 11 inches wide; binding, ½ inch wide. Yardage required: sashing and inset borders, 2¼ yards; outer borders, 3¼ yards; backing, 8 yards; binding, ¾ yard.

CUTTING SASHING AND BORDERS

I prefer to cut the sashing, borders, and background blocks before I start piecing my sampler blocks. There is a good reason for this. The sashing, borders, and background blocks take up the greatest amounts of fabric. If, after cutting these out, you feel there might not be enough fabric left for piecing, you will have time to purchase more. As with buying yarn, you cannot depend on being able to get exactly the same shade if you have to buy it at a later date. Fabric manufactureres usually make a print for only one season (three or four months). If a print is very popular, a store may have only one opportunity to buy it. This is why it is so important for you to purchase all the fabric you need at one time.

I learned this while making my first quilt. I ran out of a solid green fabric for the binding and looked for it for three years. Since the fabric was available, I knew the color was probably still being made. Five days before I was to hang my quilt in a show I found the fabric—an exact match. After that experience, I now buy all (and more) than I need to begin with.

So that you will have a specific quilt to refer to, I will use the twin to the floor layout (Fig. 4–21). Study the layout. You will see that there are four sashing strips that measures 8 by 16 inches and one long sash that is 8 by 64 inches. The inner border is the same color as the sashing and will be cut at the same time. There are two strips 8 by 56 inches and two strips 8 by 80 inches.

Note: When mentioning sizes, I *do not* include seam allowances. They are finished, sewn measurements. You must mentally add the ¼-inch seams for the cutting measurements.

Determining Cutting Methods

There are two ways to cut out your fabric (Fig. 4–22). Method 1 is to cut all pieces so the longest measurement runs the lengthwise straight-of-grain (parallel to the selvage). This eliminates any piecing of the sashing or borders, but frequently uses the most fabric. Refer to Figure 4–6.

Method 2 is more economical in fabric use. The longest measurements are placed on the crosswise straight-of-grain. The long sash and the borders would be pieced, with that seam being treated as if it didn't exist. I use both methods depending on the amount of fabric waste and how much money I have to spend on fabric. Refer to Figure 4–6.

All diagrams are figured on the use of 44-inch material—washed, dried, and selvage edge removed. Be sure to add seam allowances when figuring yardage amounts or cutting out.

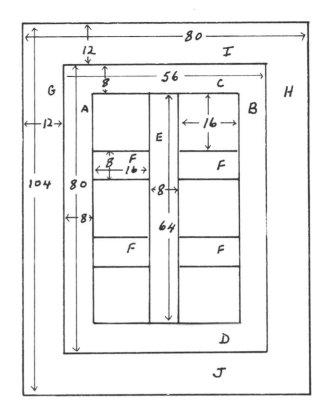

Fig. 4-21 The twin to floor layout measurements are indicated in inches. A through F are sashing and inner border units. G through J are the outer border units. These are all finished measurements. The seam allowances must be added when figuring yardage and when cutting.

Study Figure 4–21 to see how many of each unit are required. Next compare the measurements in Fig. 4–22 for cutting the sashing and inner borders (A through F). Obviously, there is an advantage in using method 1, since you won't have to do any piecing, and it only requires buying ⅛ yard more fabric.

In cutting the outer borders (G through J) in Fig. 4–23, you can readily see, by comparing methods 1 and 2, that you have to purchase over one yard more material for method 1 and will have quite a bit of leftover material. You probably will be able to use it in piecing the blocks, depending on your color scheme. Even if you can't, I would still use method 1, as it means only a difference of one yard and has the advantage of no seam lines in the borders.

These examples are really not dissimilar. I am currently making a king-size quilt in the Crossed Canoes pattern (see Fig. 12–2). The borders are white and I didn't want to piece them. From the measurements in Fig. 4–24 you can really see a dramatic difference. Method 1 means purchasing almost twice the material, with a tremendous amount of leftover fabric. Needless to say, I chose method 2.

Cutting Method 1

Cutting Method 2

Fig. 4-22 In comparing the cutting of sashing and inner borders, it is apparent that method 1 has the advantage. The units do not have to be pieced and only a small amount of extra fabric has to be purchased.

Method 1

Method 2

Fig. 4-23 In comparing methods 1 and 2 for cutting the outer borders, I would use method 1, even though there is slightly over 1 yard of extra material. The excess can be used in piecing.

Method 1

Method 2

Fig. 4-24 The cutting diagram for the border of a king-size Crossed Canoes quilt. Method 1 would not be the choice this time because of the amount of leftover fabric and the cost involved.

Top and bottom lap   Side lap

Mitered corners

Fig. 4-25 Lapped and mitered quilt corners. The shaded areas in the lapped drawings show sections that could be pieced with the outer border fabric to give a continuous band of border color.

Sashing and Border Templates

Make a template for the sashing and borders after determining the best way to cut your fabric. For the twin to the floor layout, the sash is 8 by 16 inches. Your template can be made from Mylar, manila folders, or stiff paper. I normally use artist's drawing

paper because it has some body to it yet enough light can shine through for marking quilting designs (see Chapter 7).

Make the template just as you did for the small patch templates, only work in a larger size. Lay the template on the wrong side of the fabric and trace around it with a pencil. Make sure that ½ inch is left between each pencil line for the ¼-inch seam allowances. Cut the fabric out.

CUTTING BORDER CORNERS

I have not yet dealt specifically with border corners. There are two ways to turn a corner: lap and miter. Your choice should be determined both by the interior design of the quilt and by personal preference. The lapped corners use a template with a squared end and the mitered borders use a template with a 45-degree angle end (Fig. 4-25).

A Log Cabin quilt pattern would use a lapped corner, because the blocks are made of narrow strips arranged so that the corners lap over each other. A quilt called Fragmented Star (see Fig. 8-22) would have mitered corners, since the block design has 45-degree angles in the corners. If the quilt is a sampler, there are a variety of block designs, and either lapped or mitered corners could be used, whichever you prefer. The style of corner you choose must be used throughout the quilt (Fig. 4-26). The inner border should not be lapped with a mitered outer border.

The lapped border is easier to cut, since all the ends are square. Using the twin to floor layout, decide whether you want the long laps on the sides or on the top and bottom (see Fig. 4-26). Adjust the measurements on the layout accordingly and cut the borders.

Handling mitered corners is a little more difficult. You will be dealing with 45-degree angles at the strip ends. Each strip must have a straight edge to pin into

Fig. 4-26 Compare the difference in these lapped measurements to the basic twin to floor measurements in Figure 4-21.

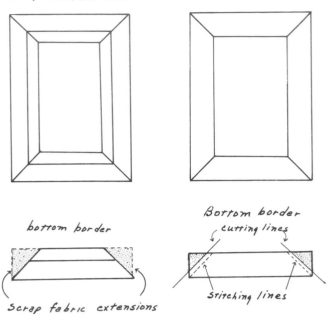

Multiple border unit

bottom border

Scrap fabric extensions

Bottom border
cutting lines

Stitching lines

Fig. 4-27 (left) The shaded areas indicate the excess fabric for single borders that will be cut away after the strip is quilted. This eliminates the need to baste on an extension. Be sure to leave a ¼-inch seam allowance when cutting.

Fig. 4-28 (right) The multiple mitered borders must be handled so that the strip end is squared off. Scrap fabric extensions (shaded areas) are basted onto the basted strip unit. The extension is removed after quilting.

the quilt-as-you-go frame, so accommodations have to be made. If the quilt is to have a single border, cut the border with a straight end. Mark the 45-degree angle stitching line on the wrong side of the fabric, just as you have for all other stitching lines. Do not cut the excess away. Assemble the strip, pin it into the frame and do the quilting. Cut the excess away after the strip is quilted and removed from the frame (Fig. 4-27).

For a multiple border, it is best to cut away the

excess material before assembling the strip. Assemble the strip with the batt and backing which are also mitered. Since you must have a straight edge to pin into the frame, an extension must be basted onto the basted strip along the 45-degree angle (Fig. 4-28). Any type of cotton-weight fabric can be used. Be sure it is basted securely to the angled cut edge. The straight edge of the extension is pinned to the frame's tape. Quilt as usual and then remove the basted fabric.

Chapter Five

Piecing and Patching

No matter how complicated the block may be, all piecing is done in the same manner. More involved blocks simply have more patches in smaller sizes and differing shapes. Once a beginning quilter has learned the few tricks to piecing, it's full steam ahead on more elaborate designs!

JOINING SINGLE EDGES

Study the photograph of the completed Miner's Lamp block in the color section, Fig. 1. Refer to Chapter 2 for color selection. Make the elongated hexagon template and cut out the fabric patches as detailed in Chapter 3. The hexagon unit is pieced beginning with the center patch and then each patch is added in order, following the numbered sequence in Fig. 5–1, until all the patches are joined. *Remember:* The pencil line on the patch is the stitching line; you *never* sew into any seam allowance as in dressmaking.

Place patches 1 and 2 with their right sides together. Pin straight into the *exact* pencil line corner of one patch and through the fabrics so that the pin comes out the other patch at its *exact* penciled corner

(Fig. 5–2). Bring the pinpoint back up through the fabric on both pencil lines.

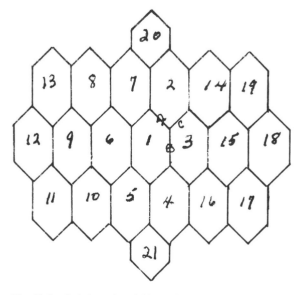

Fig. 5–1 Patches should be joined as they are numbered. Patch 3 is joined at the B edge, then flopped and joined at the C edge.

Fig. 5-2 With right sides together, pin straight into the fabrics at the penciled corners.

Fig. 5-4 The needle is brought through from the back patch and about 1/8 inch in from the penciled corner.

Pin the other end of the seam line in the same manner (Fig. 5–3). Notice that the pin heads are at the corners and that the sharp ends point toward the middle of the seam. If the patch is long, additional pins will be needed in the middle of the seam line. Be sure the pins are on the pencil lines of *both* patches.

Sewing Straight Seams

You are now ready to sew the first seam. Cut a thread about 18 inches long and knot it; use a single thread with a small knot. All thread is twisted and placed onto the spool so that there is less friction in sewing if the cut end is knotted. Hold the two patches firmly, close to the pin, between thumb and forefinger. Remove the pin and bring the needle up from the back patch so that the tip of the needle is about 1/8 inch in from the corner and on the pencil lines. Pull the thread through so that the knot is firmly against the back patch (Fig. 5–4). Now put the needle point into the *exact* corner of the top patch, making sure it comes out at the *exact* corner of the back patch. Angle the needle forward so that it comes up on the pencil lines between the corner and the thread knot (Fig. 5–5). Pull the thread through and taut. In simple terms, you have made a backstitch at the corner. You

may feel this is not necessary, but I believe it provides a little extra stability at the corners.

To sew the main portion of the seam, run the needle in and out of the fabric on both pencil lines until there are four or five stitches on the needle (Fig. 5–6). I can't stress enough how important it is to sew on the pencil lines of *both* patches. Before you pull the needle through, turn the patch over and make sure that the needle is on the pencil line of the back patch (Fig. 5–7). If it's not, pull the needle out and shift the patches until the pencil lines are exactly aligned. You must always check this, since poor alignment now will produce an inaccurate quilt.

Once you're certain of your alignment, pull the needle through and the thread taut. Quite frequently the fabric will be puckered after the needle has been pulled through. These puckers should not be left in the patch. Gently grasp the seam between thumb and forefinger and slide your fingers along the seam toward the loose end of the thread. This will remove the puckers and leave the seam flat. I do this each time I have taken four or five stitches and pulled the needle through. It should not be done at the end of the seam since it might stretch the fabric.

Fig. 5-3 Pin the patches together on the penciled lines.

Fig. 5-5 Stitch directly into the penciled corners on *both* patches and bring the needle back up on the lines. This makes a backstitch at the corner for extra stability.

Fig. 5-6 The needle is moved in and out on *both* pencil lines until four or five stitches are picked up. Stitches should be no longer than 1/16 of an inch.

Fig. 5-7 Turn the patch over *before* pulling the needle through the fabric to see if the needle is on the pencil line of the back patch. If not, pull the needle out, shift the fabric to align the pencil lines and restitch.

Fig. 5-8 When ending the running stitch, make a backstitch right into the corner of the patch for added strength. *Do not* stitch into the seam allowance.

Fig. 5-9 To make a knot, put the needle through the top of a figure 8 thread loop and bring it out the bottom loop. Pull tight and cut, leaving a ¼-inch tail.

Continue the running stitch until close to the end of the seam. Hold the fabric firmly, remove the pin, and stitch right into the corner point. Make a small backstitch and come back up at the corner (Fig. 5-8).

To knot the thread, pick up a few threads of the patch just inside the seam allowance area and pull the thread through until a small loop is made. The loop should form a figure 8. If it has not done so, use the tip of the needle to twist the thread into an 8. Put the needle through the top loop of the figure 8 and out the bottom loop (Fig. 5-9). Pull the thread taut so that a firm knot forms. Cut the thread off, leaving a thread tail of ⅛ to ¼ inch. If the thread were cut right next to the knot it might come loose. I've found that the figure 8 knot makes a very firm, tight knot, but if you prefer another type, that's okay too.

JOINING MULTIPLE EDGES (Flopping)

While it is easy to join two patches that have straight edges, it's a bit more difficult to be able to sew in two or more edges of the next patch without having to knot and cut the thread at each seam end. Patches 1 and 2 have been joined at seam A (see Fig. 5-1). Patch 3 must be joined at seams B and C. Place patch 3 over patch 2, right sides together, and pin on the pencil lines as detailed above. This time the pin on the left will be going into the *hole* where the last joining stitch was taken. *Note:* Never, at any time, are seam allowances to be sewn down. They are held up and out of the way when sewing. If the seam allowances are sewn down, they can't be moved when pressing.

Sew from the pin on the right to the pin on the left, making the backstitch through the same hole that ended the seam joining patches 1 and 2 (Fig. 5-10). If you are left-handed, reverse the directions and sew from left to right. Always sew from the outer corner to the patch center when joining multiple edges.

When you come to a seam allowance, hold it up and out of the way and poke the needle through it right at the stitching line. Pull the needle and thread out the other side of the seam allowance (Fig. 5-11). In this manner, you have sewn from one patch to another, but not into the seam allowances. The seam allowances are still "moveable."

I call this method of sewing multiple edges "flopping." First, one seam line is pinned and sewn; then the needle is run through the seam allowance to the other side and a backstitch is made (Fig. 5-12). Second, the end seam corner is pinned and sewn (Fig. 5-13). It would not only be very awkward to try to pin all the edges to be sewn at once; it would also produce a sloppy looking block. Using the "flopping" method, two or three edges of a square may be sewn into a block without cutting a thread.

PRESSING

Proper pressing is as important for an accurate quilt as proper piecing. Notice that I said *pressing*, not *ironing!* Pressing is a gentle action with a soft touch and as little back-and-forth motion with the iron as possible. It is very easy to stretch those tiny bias pieces of fabric and undo all that careful cutting and piecing.

Fig. 5-10 Sew up to the seam corner and make a backstitch into the hole where the last stitch was taken to join patches 1 and 2. The patch edge has been folded back and a pin inserted under the thread to show this.

Fig. 5-11 The needle is put through the seam allowance at stitching-line level. This leaves the seam allowance free to be moved when pressing.

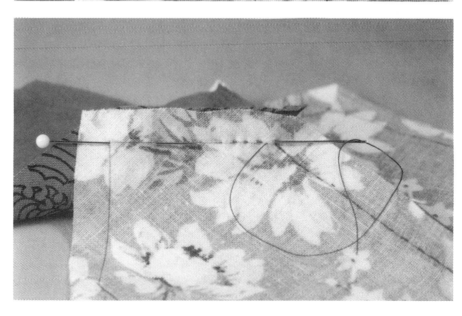

Fig. 5-12 Flop the patch being added up to match the penciled corner. Pin that corner and backstitch at the corner you just stitched for added strength.

Fig. 5-13 Continue sewing the seam line to the end. End the seam as usual by backstitching and knotting.

Any iron can be used, either steam or dry. A number of years ago, I got tired of my steam iron burping out brown spots on the fabric. I gave that iron to my sons to hot wax their skis and bought a dry iron and a spray bottle to spritz water, but have since returned to a steam iron of a different type. I now have a tailor's gravity feed iron. This iron is much heavier and produces large quantities of steam (be careful of steam burns). Though expensive, this iron does a wonderful job in compressing multiple seam allowances. Whatever your choice, have the soleplate clean and use new water each time so no spotting occurs. Be sure to select the correct temperatures for the fabric content, and if the fabric becomes shiny, use a pressing cloth.

Seams in quilting are *never* pressed open, but to one side. If the seams are pressed open, as in dressmaking, the thread is exposed to extra tension and wear (Fig. 5–14a). When seams are pressed to one side, the top patch will roll over the bottom patch very slightly and protect the seam thread (Fig. 5–14b).

When piecing, it is best to press as you go. I generally piece similar units in a block design, stop, press them and then continue piecing. It makes the pressing and piecing easier, especially if you're working on a block with lots of tiny pieces. And the end product will look more finished.

With the hexagon unit, I suggest piecing the center (1) and the first row (2 to 7), then press seam allowances before continuing the piecing. Lay the pieced unit, seams up, on the edge of the ironing board, with part of the unit hanging over the edge. This allows only one area to be pressed and simplifies the job (Fig.

5–15). Press the center patch (1) so that the seam allowances lie flat and are not folded back onto the patch. At the same time, the seams in the first row are pressed so that they all go in the same direction (Fig. 5–16).

A general rule to follow when pressing a block is to try not to turn the allowances toward each other, especially if they are very close, as in a diamond point. In very complicated blocks this may not be possible, and you may even have to change direction of the seam midway on the seam line, but do this only if there is no other alternative.

Now rotate the unit so that the area already pressed hangs off the ironing board and finish the

Fig. 5-14a If patch seams are pressed open, the thread is exposed to friction and additional tension.

Fig. 5-14b Seams pressed to one side make the top patch roll over the bottom patch, thus protecting the thread.

Fig. 5-15 Place the block, or a section of it, wrong side up on the ironing board. Press only a small portion of the block at any time. Let the rest hang over the ironing board.

Fig. 5-16 The center patch is pressed with seams flat, and the remaining rows are pressed with seams all lying in the same direction.

Fig. 5-17 Turn the unit right side up and re-press each seam. Frequently the seams overlap and thus must be eliminated. A pin is in the fold for illustration.

Fig. 5-18 A pleat is formed at the corners when the outer hexagons are pressed.

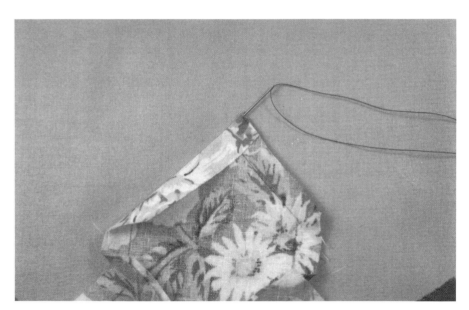

Fig. 5-19 Place the needle on the pencil line and fold the seam allowance back over the needle. Hold the folded seam allowance in place and remove the needle.

Fig. 5-20 Place the needle along the converging pencil line and fold that seam allowance over the needle. Hold the folded seam allowance in place, remove the needle, and baste the seam allowance.

pressing. Turn the block right side up and re-press each seam. This is very important since the seams have frequently overlapped each other (Fig. 5–17).

Continue piecing the outer row of patches (8 to 19) to the unit that you just pressed. When completed, the seam allowances should be pressed in the same direction as the first row you pressed. Piece the small outer hexagons to the unit, and press them so that a pleat forms at the point of the hexagons where they join the larger hexagons (Fig. 5–18).

BASTING

The Miner's Lamp hexagon unit has now been pieced and is almost ready to be appliqued to the background block; however, the outer, raw edges must first be turned under on the pencil lines and basted down. Since the pencil lines are on the wrong sides of the patches, you will need to peek under the edges as you turn them to make sure the fold is on the line. As you turn under the seams, baste them in place with

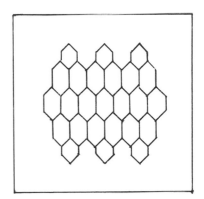

Fig. 5-21 The pieced unit can bo made with either two or six of the smaller hexagons. It is then appliqued to the background block.

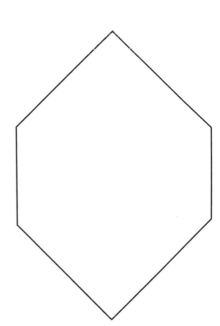

Fig. 5-22 Pattern for the Miner's Lamp block.

white thread (basting thread, if you have it). Don't use colored thread, as it may leave dye marks when pulled out. To get a sharp-cornered turn, place the needle right on the pencil line and fold the fabric over the needle (Fig. 5–19). Hold the seam in place and remove the needle. Now put the needle along the pencil line on the next edge, and fold that seam allowance down (Fig. 5–20). Baste in place. Continue to baste around the entire unit.

Contrary to every book you've ever read about applique, do not press the basted edges! If they are pressed down, any basting inaccuracy will be "nailed" in. I would then defy anyone to try to make a correction, short of removing all basting and starting over. Using my method of applique, you will never press any applique, and only on the Miner's Lamp will you even do any basting. Trust me. It might take you a little longer to learn, but it will really increase your applique speed and, more importantly, you will produce superior applique.

Chapter Six

Block Assembly

Researchers believe that the first pieced quilts were made of patches of all the same size and shape. Certainly, it would have been easy and fast to cut out similar shapes from scrap fabric and sew them together. But I can imagine that, after making several of these, a woman might have become bored with such a necessary, repetitious occupation and would have tried to make it more interesting. Since her color selection was probably very limited, she may well have decided to create more interest by cutting the simple shapes apart into various new units, which may have developed into the patterns we are familar with today (Fig. 6-1).

Because the unit divisions in Fig. 6-1 are easy to make by folding paper or fabric, they probably formed the basis for the first quilt blocks. As more

Fig. 6-1 (a) "Simple repeat," square block arrangement; (b) "four patch," dividing the square into four equal divisions; (c) "nine patch," the block divided into 9 equal divisions; (d) "nine patch," the block divided into 9 unequal parts.

a

b

c

d

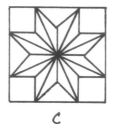

Fig. 6-2 (a) Five-unit division, Monkey Wrench pattern; (b) seven-unit division, Bear's Paw pattern; (c) diamond division, Lemoyne Star pattern.

Fig. 6-3 Blocks with many patches still fall into basic categories: (a) "four patch," Mixed T; (b) "five patch," Joseph's Coat; (c) "seven patch," Pine Tree; (d) "nine patch," Noon Lily.

creative hands worked at quilting, block divisions become more complicated and more difficult to draw and cut accurately. The blocks in the following figures are divided into five and seven units (Fig. 6-2). Diamond patterns can be the most involved to draft accurately and fall into their own classification.

In any of the block categories in Figures 6-1 and 6-2, each of the small units can be divided into smaller shapes to give an infinite variety to a block design. Even so, that block would still keep its original classification. It is important to note that some blocks have so many divisions that it may be difficult to decide just which group they fall into (Fig. 6-3).

In this chapter we will discuss piecing a basic "four patch" combined with an easy applique design, the Dancing Flame. Regardless of the shape of the patches, all piecing is done as described in Chapter 5, Figures 5-2 through 5-13. For that reason, in this and succeeding chapters, I will only deal with specific problems in constructing a block.

METHODS OF ASSEMBLY

Once you have become comfortable with the mechanics of piecing, each new block design offers a challenge in choosing fabrics and colors as well as in their placement and block assembly. If three people piece

the same block, they each may put it together in a different order. All would be correct, but one way might be the easiest. Study each block and try to determine which way will be the easiest for you. In the simpler blocks, such as Dancing Flame, there would be few alternatives in the piecing sequence. Refer to 6-4 for the Dancing Flame assembly. Also see color Fig. 1.

In more complicated blocks, like Twisted Bands, a nine-patch, there can be more than one way to assemble it. The method I have diagrammed is the easiest

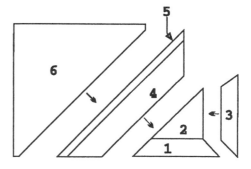

Fig. 6-4 One-quarter assembly of Dancing Flame. Repeat three more times, then join the four quarters as detailed in Fig. 8-6.

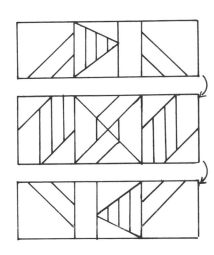

Fig. 6-5 This seems to be the easiest way to assemble Twisted Bands. (See Fig. 8-21 for the pattern.)

for me (Fig. 6–5), but after studying the block, you may find one or two other choices. Study color Fig. 2.

To simplify piecing, I recommend all like units be assembled at the same time. For Twisted Bands, first piece all the triangular units and narrow strips, then piece them with the larger patches into small blocks. Next, join the small blocks into strips or rows and then the rows into the completed block.

Whichever method is used to join the blocks, all corners should meet perfectly and all seam allowances should be movable for pressing. Refer to Figs. 5–10 to 5–13.

SIMPLE APPLIQUE: DANCING FLAME

The applique of the flame shapes to the block should be done only after the piecing of the entire block is completed. Attempting to applique onto small patches might result in pulling the fabric out of shape. Besides, it's just simply easier to handle the larger block.

Note: Marking for the applique locations, however, should be done *before* any block assembly occurs. The order is: mark and cut out the patches, mark applique lines on the necessary patches, assemble the block, applique where needed.

In Miner's Lamp, the pieced unit was positioned in the center of the background block and checked by ruler to make sure that it was properly aligned. Because you were only dealing with a single finished

shape on a single background, that method was adequate. The Dancing Flame is a different matter.

SIMPLE MASTER PATTERN

There are four flame shapes to be appliqued onto four background patches. If you used the "plunk and pin" method favored in most books on applique, you would not have each of the four shapes in exact finished size, pointed in exactly the same direction or positioned in precisely the same spot. *This is important.*

There is a very simple, effective way to handle applique in this situation. On each of the patch templates that has an applique, draw the finished-size design in the exact location you want it. This has been done for you on the Dancing Flame pattern (Fig. 6–8). Do not include the seam allowances. To make a simple master pattern, cut out the template (Fig. 6–6) as usual. Make a copy of your template from typing paper or paper of a similar weight. Duplicate the flame design by laying the paper over the template and tracing over the flame shape. Go over this penciled line with dark, felt-tip pen; a ball-point pen might smear. You have just made a very simple paper master pattern.

Place the paper master pattern on the *wrong* side of the fabric patch, being careful to match its edges to the penciled stitching lines. Pin in place. Tape this small, pinned unit to the window (paper touching

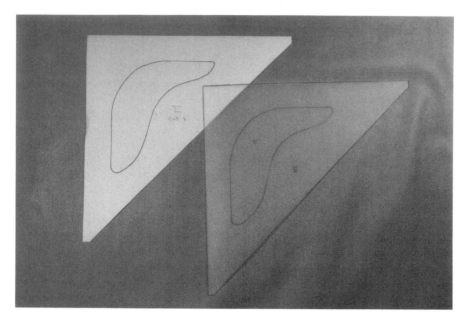

Fig. 6-6 The finished acetate and master templates for Dancing Flame. The paper master is made from the acetate pattern. (Edges have been outlined for photographic clarity.)

Fig. 6-7 A small portion of Victorian Wicker master laid on the background block. Notice the fineness of the penciled line.

glass). The right side of the fabric is facing you. The light will shine through the fabric well enough that you will be able to see the darkened pencil line. This will be the stitching line for the applique, so make sure the lines are dark and unbroken. Refer to Figures 7–6 and 7–7. Press the pencil onto the fabric just hard enough so that the line will be visible on the fabric. It takes some practice, since you can't really see the line as you draw it because of the dark pen line underneath. Try it out on a scrap of fabric first. See Fig. 6–7. If you are using a white or light-colored fabric, the marking can probably be done on a tabletop. For a more detailed explanation of this technique and for the actual Dancing Flame applique instructions, see Chapter 7.

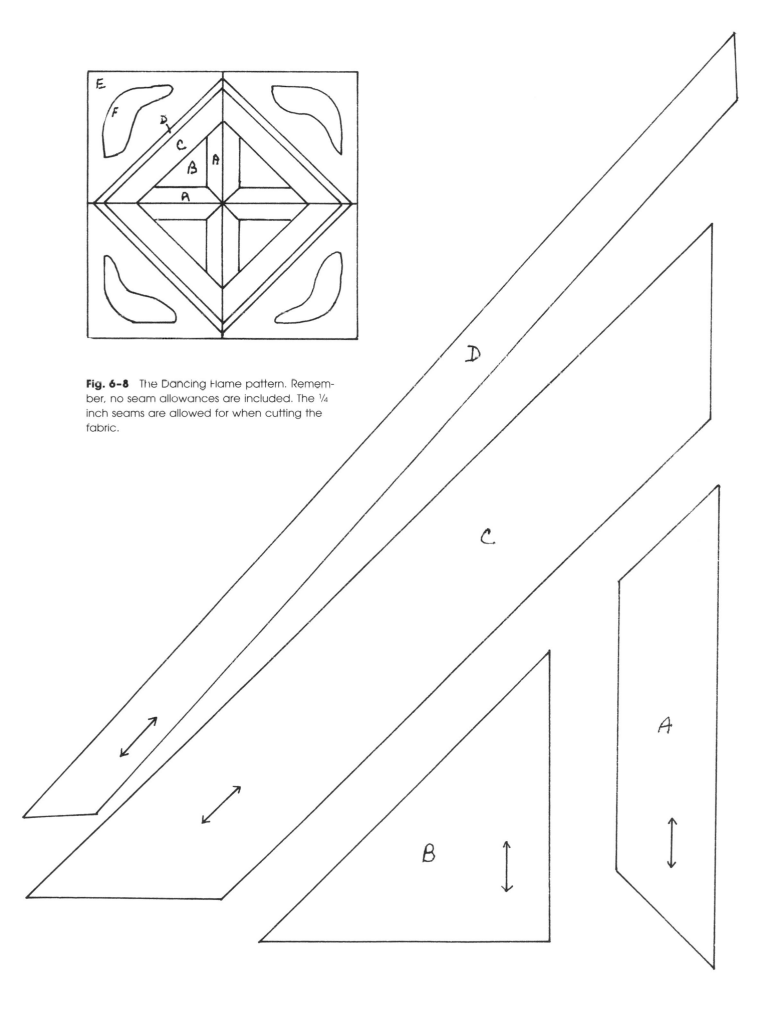

Fig. 6-8 The Dancing Flame pattern. Remember, no seam allowances are included. The ¼ inch seams are allowed for when cutting the fabric.

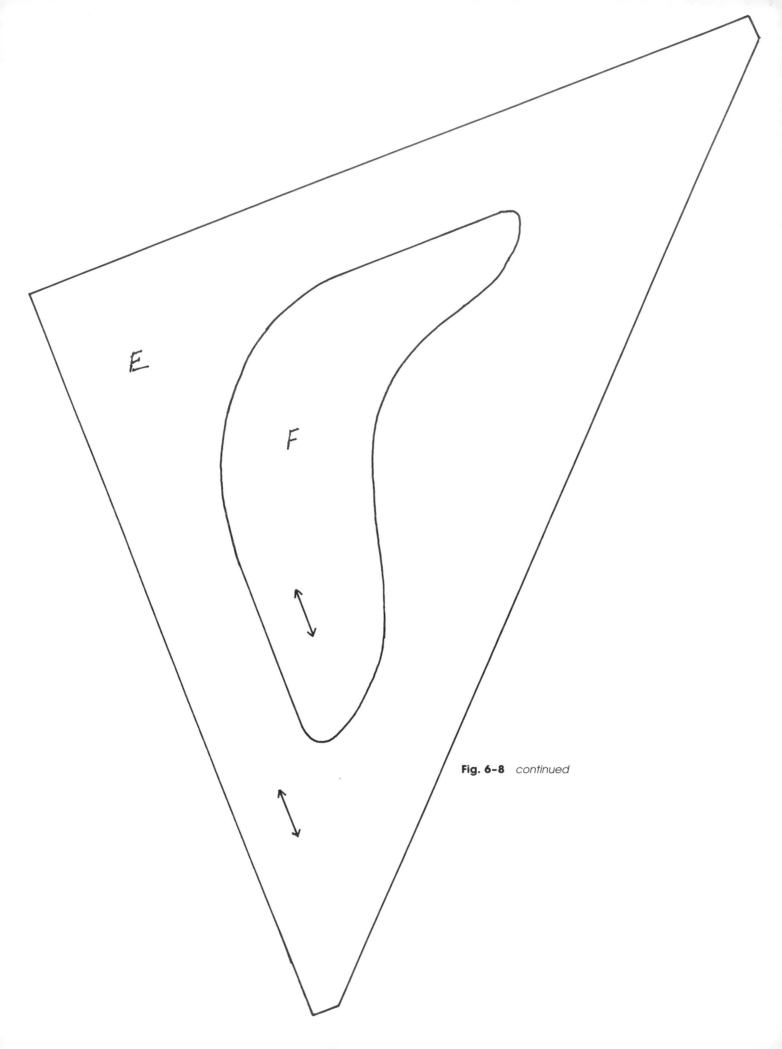

Fig. 6-8 *continued*

Chapter Seven

Easy, Accurate Applique

Applique—to me, the most exciting, creative, fast, satisfying needle-and-thread technique. To many, the most frustrating, time consuming, and difficult task they ever tried.

Everything written about applique tells you to work the same way: trace around the template, cut out the fabric, baste the edges under, press, plunk down, pin in place, applique. Using my method you will make a master pattern, make the template, trace around the template, cut out the fabric, place the master pattern on the background fabric, pin the patches in place (if desired) and applique. Notice that in my method you do not do any basting or pressing and you are appliqueing to a pattern.

I want to briefly review the traditional applique method so that you understand the differences in the two methods; I then want you to promptly forget the traditional method and try the master pattern technique.

TRADITIONAL APPLIQUE

A template is made. For purposes of illustrations, we'll call it a tulip design. It is placed on the *right* side of the tulip fabric and is traced with a pencil. This is the actual, finished size of the flower. The tulip is cut out, leaving a ¼-inch seam allowance outside the pencil line. The seam allowance is turned under on the pencil line and basted in place. The basted tulip is pressed. It is then placed on the background block and moved around until it looks as if it is positioned accurately. The fabric tulip is pinned in place and appliqued. The basting threads are removed.

Let's look at some of the problems in the above method. Because the tulip design is traced onto the right side of the fabric patch, the pencil lines are often visible at the edge of the patch, even after appliqueing. Next is basting: basting stitches should be fairly long, but it is almost impossible to take even ¼-inch stitches around the curved tulip base and get a smoothly turned edge. What you will get is a series of little points on the curve. The patch is then pressed, effectively locking in all the little points. Now you must position the patch by using the "plunk and pin" method. There may be no problem if it is only one tulip on a single block; but what if you are making twelve blocks with three tulips each? It is humanly impossible to be accurate on each of the twelve blocks. That is important to me! If the quilt is all the same block design, I want all the blocks to be the same! Finally, the tulip is pinned in place and appliqued.

MASTER PATTERN APPLIQUE

Because of the problems discussed, I developed the master pattern technique. It is my hope that this method will produce superior applique with little frustration.

In almost all applique (except free-form) there is a specific design to be followed. The single-shape Dancing Flame design was discussed in Chapter 6. Other designs, like Victorian Wicker (color Fig. 1), or the Orchard Ribbons (color Fig. 3) blocks have more involved shapes, all of which must be positioned accurately. The central anchor shapes in Victorian Wicker must form a square, not be lopsided or oval, and the points should all be the same length and curve the same way. The best way to assure this is to make an accurate paper pattern for your design. This way you can do all the positioning with a pencil on paper instead of fabric patches on a background block. It's a lot faster and certainly easier to make corrections with an eraser.

Drawing the Master Pattern

Cut a piece of paper to exact finished size. Drawing paper or typing paper can be taped together to give the size you need to work with. In this book all blocks are 16-inch squares. Make sure that the square is really accurate. Begin the master by dividing the 16-

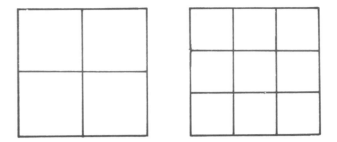

Fig. 7-1 Divide the accurate square into equal parts; these will vary, depending on the pattern.

inch square into four equal units. In this block it would be 8-inch squares (Fig. 7–1). Draw and cut out the shapes you have in mind, such as anchor shapes and outer wicker canes in Victorian Wicker, in paper without seam allowances. Move them around in one of the 8-inch squares until you are satisfied with the balance (Fig. 7–2). Trace around each shape with a pencil. This completes one quarter of the master pattern. I provide the quarter masters for all the applique blocks in this book (Figs. 7–32 and 7–33).

Now fold the paper block in half along the division line, with the design lines to the outside (Fig. 7–3). Tape the folded block to a window with the penciled design touching the glass (Fig. 7–4). Trace over the lines showing through the paper so that the design is put on the adjoining quarter section. One-half of the master pattern is completed. Open up the 16-inch paper block and fold it horizontally on the center division line. Again, tape it to a window with the penciled design touching the glass. The design can be

Fig. 7-2 Move the paper cutouts around until the design is balanced. Trace around each shape onto the graph paper.

Fig. 1 Full-size sampler quilt made by the author. Block patterns from top, left to right, are: Twisted Bands. Horizon Star, Orchard Ribbons; Jeweled Sun, Spinning Comet, Beacon Fire; Victorian Wicker, Miner's Lamp, Dancing Flame.

Fig. 2 Twisted Bands: Visualize how the strong-colored vertical and horizontal patches develop secondary patterns in block-to-block assembly.

Fig. 3 Orchard Ribbons: Advanced applique block.

Fig. 4 Spinning Comet: Note how the center patches are asymmetrical circles.

Fig. 5 Horizon Star: An exercise in assembly, as many of the patches are unequal triangles.

Fig. 6 Twisted Bands wall hanging by Marcelle Weigandt, 42 ×42. Compare how the color choices and the quarter-turn block rotation affect the secondary pattern in this block-to-block assembly.

Fig. 7 Jeweled Sun wall hanging by Monica Mitchell, 21 ×21.

Fig. 8 Dancing Flame by Nancy Lord, 15¾ × 31½. The block has been put on point and the applique "flame" eliminated, which creates a very different appearance.

Fig. 9 Quilter's color wheel with a 14-inch quilting hoop used as a frame (see Chapter 2).

Fig. 10 Fragmented Star block in a variety of color arrangements. Study which colors come forward and which recede.

Fig. 11 Pencil-colored drawing of Raindrops.

Fig. 12 Beginning of the color selection for Raindrops. The patches are pinned to a Styrofoam insulating board. Compare the color sample pinned in the corner of the board against the actual fabric choices.

Fig. 13 Raindrops wall hanging made by the author, 24½×39.

Fig. 14 Pencil-colored drawing of Forest Spheres, prior to applique changes.

Fig. 15 Forest Spheres wall hanging made by the author, 18 × 39. Machine quilted with clear nylon thread on the top and matching thread for the backing.

Fig. 7-3 Fold the penciled paper block in half with the design to the outside.

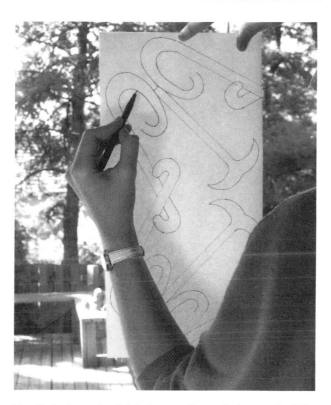

Fig. 7-4 Tape the folded paper to a window so that the penciled design touches the glass. Trace over the design showing through from the other side. A light box can also be used.

traced onto this half of the paper. Open up the paper block and the entire design is completed.

Check the design to see if you are pleased with it. Does it have any gaping holes where there should be a design motif? Is it balanced? If you need to make adjustments, work with a quarter of the design and repeat Figures 7–3 and 7–4. When the penciled design is precisely the way you want it, carefully go over each line with a fine-pointed, dark, felt-tip pen. Do not use a ball-point pen, as it might smear. The master pattern is completed.

You can use your master pattern for one block or a hundred. Don't throw it away when the block is finished; save if for future use. You can also make masters for the quilting designs on blocks, borders, and sashing of quilts, applique designs on clothing, or decorator items or for any item where a consistent pattern is needed.

Using the Master Pattern
The master pattern, for both applique and quilting designs, is used in the following manner. Cut out the background fabric in the desired shape, in this case a 16-inch square background block. Place the fabric, wrong side up, on a table. Position the master pattern, right side down, on the fabric. Align the edges of the master with the penciled stitching lines of the background block. Pin the two units together (Fig. 7–5).

Tape the pinned unit to a window with the background block fabric facing you (wrong side of the

paper touching the glass). Using a very sharp, soft-lead pencil, trace over the lines that are now visible because of light shining through the window (Fig. 7–6). This won't work at night unless a light is directed in the window from the outside. If you have a glass-topped table, place a lamp underneath the glass and it will make an instant light box. A piece of Plexiglas stretched between two chairs or beds with a light underneath will also work well.

When tracing, one tends to scratch back and forth along the line. Try to avoid this by using your wrist as a pivot point as it rests against the fabric. Draw one fine line. As you come to the end of your reach, move your hand farther along (Fig. 7–7). Again, all traced lines must be fine, solid lines that are just dark enough to be seen. I would suggest that you make a sample before working on good fabric (see Fig. 6–7).

It is important to note that at the time the master pattern is made the quilting lines can be drawn in addition to all applique locations. A master can be made for applique only, for applique and quilting design or only for quilting designs. Quilting lines should be drawn with a fine, light, solid line, not a broken line.

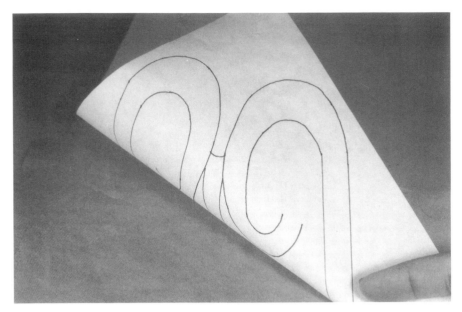

Fig. 7-5 After the penciled design is complete, put the background block, wrong side up, on a table and lay the master pattern, design side down, over it. Align the master edges to the penciled stitching lines of the background block. Pin together.

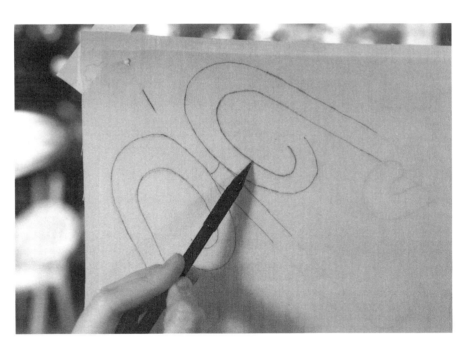

Fig. 7-6 Tape the pinned unit, paper touching glass, to a window, or use a light box. Use a very light, single line when marking the fabric. Note: Lines have been darkened for photographic clarity. Your lines *must not* be this dark.

right

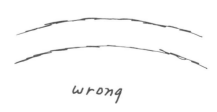

wrong

Fig. 7-7 Draw a single, fine line using your wrist as a pivot point. *Do not* scratch back and forth as you trace.

RULES FOR APPLIQUE

There are several basic rules in applique that should be followed no matter how the applique is to be used.

1. Always begin with the shape most distant and work to the foreground. *Example:* to applique a sitting dog, apply the pieces in the following order: tail, hind legs, body, front legs, head, ears, nose.

2. If two pieces of applique butt against each other, the raw edge of the patch farthest away does not have to be turned under. *Example:* to applique a butterfly, sew on both wings, but do not turn under the edges that will connect to the body. Applique the body over the wing seam allowances.

3. For hand work, always use a single thread with a color that matches the fabric of the applique patch. *Example:* for a red flower on a white background block, use red thread.

4. When appliqueing a tree or flower stem and leaves, the main trunk is always appliqued last. *Example:* the smallest branches of a tree are appliqued first. The end seam allowances are then covered by the next larger branches. This progression continues until the largest branches are sewn on, and their end seam allowances are covered by the tree trunk. In nature, the branches closest to you would join with the front surface of the trunk; with applique, however, we are dealing only with a flat surface. In addition, it's just neater to end the branches behind the trunk.

5. If possible, never start appliqueing at or near a corner, at a point, or at the height or depth of a curve.

Try to start in an area that is as straight as possible. Of course, with a circle, it won't make any difference.

6. Use the needle as a turning tool for folding under seam allowances. Do not use your fingers.

7. *Never* trim seam allowances ahead of time. Trim only the area immediately in front of where you are actually appliqueing.

STRAIGHT LINE APPLIQUE: MINER'S LAMP

When an applique design changes fabric colors at the outer edges, as in Miner's Lamp, it is not necessary to change thread at each fabric patch. Choose the thread color that best matches the hexagon colors and the background color. However, if you are using strong, contrasting colors like red, white, and blue, you may feel it is best to change thread at each patch. This will take a little longer, but you will be more pleased with the results.

To begin the applique, use as fine a "sharp" or embroidery needle as you can thread (see Chapter 1, under Supplies). I use a #10 "sharp" for all piecing and applique. Use a single thread, no longer than 12 to 15 inches, with a small knot. Bring the needle under the edge of the applique unit and up to the surface, just catching the edge of the hexagon (Fig. 7–8). Insert the needle into the background fabric just beside the thread that is coming out of the applique patch. Angle the needle forward a scant ¼ inch, bring the needle tip up through the background block and catch the edge of the applique patch. Bring the needle to the surface of the block and pull the thread taut

Fig. 7-8 To start applique, bring the needle, with a single, knotted thread, up under the very edge of the applique patch to the surface. Pull the knot firmly against the back of the Miner's Lamp fabric.

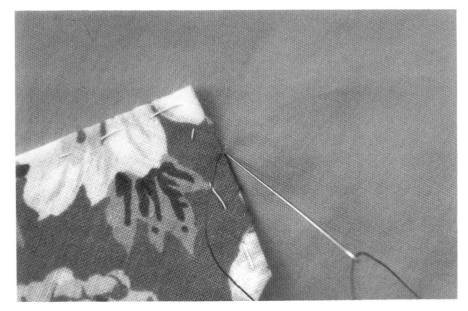

Fig. 7-9 The needle's tip goes into the background block directly opposite the thread coming out of the patch, whatever its shape. Angle the needle forward a scant ¼ inch and come back up through the background block and the edge of the patch. Pull the thread taut. Repeat around the patch. A long stitch will show on the wrong side of the background block. (See Fig. 7-11.)

Fig. 7-10 Stitch right into the corner point of each hexagon. These corners must be "nailed down."

(Fig. 7–9). Repeat the above step around the appliqued edges. At each of the hexagon corners, take a stitch right into the point; this will make a sharp corner and hold it firmly in place (7–10).

Ending Applique Threads

When the thread ends or the entire design has been sewn down, take the needle to the back of the background block and pull all the thread through. Catch a few threads of the background block, just inside the stitching line. Pull the thread enough so that a loop of about ½ inch is left (Fig. 7–11). Knot and cut the thread. Refer to Fig. 5–9 for knots.

Next, put the needle tip into the space between the background block and the applique unit. Bring the tip of the needle out about ¼ inch away. Pull the thread through and cut if off at the surface of the fabric (Fig. 7–12). The thread tail will drop into the area between the background block and the applique and be hidden. The thread tail should not be visible. This is especially important if the background block is a light color and the thread is dark. If the thread were simply cut off, the tail would be visible from the surface of the block. My method is neater! The Miner's Lamp block is now completed and can be put aside until you are ready to assemble it into the strip for quilting.

Fig. 7-11 Catch a few threads of the background block just inside the stitching line. Pull the thread through until a ½ inch figure 8 loop is formed. Make a knot as in Figure 5-9.

INTRICATE APPLIQUE: VICTORIAN WICKER

At the beginning of this chapter you used a master pattern to trace the applique design onto the background block. The individual applique patches should be cut out in the same manner as patches for geometric piecing, i.e., trace the pattern onto the wrong side of the fabric using a template and cut ¼ inch outside the pencil line to leave a seam allowance. *Note:* These pencil lines are only a guide for cutting. They are to be ignored once appliqueing begins.

Remember, the actual applique stitch is the same for all applique, whether the patches are straight or curved. Refer back to Fig. 7-8 to 7-12, if you need to review.

Place the central anchor-shaped patch (Fig. 7-32A) right side up over one of the anchor outlines on the prepared background block. Lift up the patch edges to make sure that it is centered and that there is adequate seam allowance on all sides. Pin the patch to the background block. Once you become adept at this applique techinque, you won't need to pin very small patches.

Starting at midpoint on one of the long, straight edges, applique *toward* the anchor's curved fluke end (Fig. 7-13). Trim the seam allowance as you applique to a scant ¼ inch. Don't trim the entire patch ahead of time. You could cut too much off and have to start over. Make sure you sew to the pencil line on the background block; this is your pattern. Ignore the line on the wrong side of the patch, it was only a guide for cutting the patch out.

Fig. 7-12 Work the needle between the background block and the patch for about ½ inch. Pull the thread out of the background block and cut the thread off at the fabric's surface. The thread tail will drop between the two layers of fabric and be hidden.

Fig. 7-13 Turn the seam allowance under with the needle's tip. *Do not* turn any seams with your fingers. Using the needle as a turning tool may be awkward, but once mastered it will increase the speed of applique.

Points

To make a sharp point, take a stitch into the patch directly over the penciled point on the background block. All the seam allowance is now pointing to the unsewn side of the anchor's fluke. Place the point of the needle into the front edge of the seam allowance and push it back into the fold of the fabric (Fig. 7–14) so that it rests against the seam line (Fig. 7–15). Take a stitch into the background block at the very point of the anchor's tip so that it is sewn firmly in place (Fig. 7–16).

If necessary, trim away some of the top and bottom seam allowances. There should be enough fabric left to make the fold, but not enough to prevent a fine, sharp point from being formed (Fig. 7–17). Place the needle tip into the trimmed seam allowance and push it under. The side of the needle is used as a "pusher." Study Figs. 7–18 and 7–19 for this technique. Take a stitch very close to the anchor's fluke tip and then continue appliqueing around the convex curve of the anchor, repeating the point turning directions at the anchor's other fluke tip (Fig. 7–20).

Fig. 7-14 Use the tip of the needle to push the point of the fabric back into the fold of the patch's seam.

Fig. 7-15 Press the needle back into the fold of the fabric.

Fig. 7-16 Take a stitch into the background block and up through the very point of the patch. The point will be ''nailed down'' with this stitch.

Fig. 7-17 Trim seams, if necessary. If too much fabric is left, the point will be bulky.

Fig. 7-18 The fabric is shoved under with the needle's tip.

Fig. 7-19 Use the side of the needle to finish pushing the seam allowance under the patch.

Fig. 7-20 Take another stitch at the patch's point as in Figure 7-16 and continue appliqueing down the side of the patch. Trim excess seam allowance just ahead of where you are appliqueing.

Curves (Concave and Convex)

It is not difficult to applique a tight curve. Here are some basic rules you'll need to remember when working with curves:

1. Concave seam allowances should be clipped so the seam can stretch (Fig. 7–21).

2. Cut V shapes out of convex seam allowances to remove excess fabric when folding it under (Fig. 7–21).

3. The tighter the curve, the closer the stitches should be.

4. Seam allowances should be trimmed to about ⅛ inch, but trim only ½ inch ahead of where you are stitching.

The secret to making smooth curves is to fold the seam allowance under only about ⅓ inch ahead of the last stitch taken (Fig. 7–22). Roll the seam allowance under with the needle tip so that the edge is smooth. You may have to shift the folded seam allowance a bit to get an even curve. If there is a tiny point that won't go away, take a stitch right into its point. You'll find that the point will disappear when the thread is pulled tight.

Fig. 7-21 Clip concave curves and take small V shapes out of convex curves. Note: Pencil lines were darkened for photographic clarity.

Fig. 7-22 Only work about ⅓ inch at a time when appliqueing curves.

Continue appliqueing around the curves and up the straight side of the anchor, back to where the applique began, folding in the narrow top edge when sewing. End the thread as directed in Figs. 7–11 and 7–12.

It may take some time for you to master the technique of handling the needle as a turning tool, but I believe you will enjoy the speed and ease of applique once you have practiced a bit.

Straight and Curved Stems

The following techniques apply to both narrow and wide strips of fabric. If a line is even slightly curved, the fabric must be cut on the bias so that it will "move" when being sewn. The fabric may be cut on the straight-of-grain if the design is in a straight line.

Traditional Stem Applique.   If stems are ¼ inch or more in width, first turn one raw edge under and applique, then fold the remaining raw edge under and applique it. You can also baste both edges under and then applique the stem one side at a time. It is important to note, if the stem is curved, the inside curve must be sewn first (Fig. 7–23). If the outside curve is sewn first, the inside curve will pucker.

You are using a master pattern with this applique and are sewing to pencil lines. Do not baste under the seam allowances on the fabric strip. If basted, the fabric won't be adjustable.

Nontraditional Stem Applique. I found the above method especially awkward, actually impossible, when working with very narrow stems where the edges are trimmed so much that they begin to fray. So I developed another method, which I subsequently found on quilts dating from the 1930s. I'm sure others have used this method, but I've never found it discussed in any book.

Note: The Victorian Wicker master pattern is *not* being used for the following stem applique technique, since it does not apply to the pattern. However, this technique is used when appliqueing stems, branches or long, narrow, curving shapes. There is no pattern included.

Cut out a fabric curve. It usually will not be on a true bias, but will be flexible enough to work with. Lay the fabric, wrong side up, over the penciled stem line on the background block. The outer (bigger) curved line of the patch should lie over the outer curved line of the master (Fig 7–24). *Do not pin it to the background block.* Note how the fabric patch curves away from the master lines. Using a single, knotted thread, sew the outer line of the patch to the outer line of the master with a tiny running stitch. If you are appliqueing a stem that will have an end covered with another shape, a flower for this example, then allow at least ¼ inch seam allowance to extend under the flower (see Fig. 7–24 for the placement).

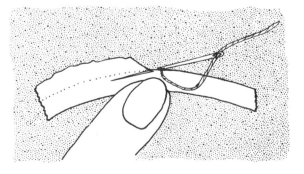

Fig. 7-23 Always applique inside (concave) curves first. The dashed line indicates the stitching line of the master pattern on the background fabric.

Fig. 7-24 Place the stem's greatest curve, wrong side up, over the greatest penciled curve on the background block. The patch will curve away from the master line. Note: Pencil lines are darkened for photographic clarity in this series of examples.

Start the running stitch in the end seam allowance (Fig. 7-25). Take three or four stitches on the needle each time and then pull the thread through. Put the needle tip into the stem patch seam allowance about ⅓ inch ahead of the last stitch and shift the fabric over enough so that the two pencil lines align, one atop the other (Fig. 7-26). The pencil line will not be visible on the master, so fold the fabric stem back on itself to see if the needle has been placed accurately (Fig. 7-27). If so, pull the thread through. If not, remove the needle, reposition the fabric stem and sew

again. Continue sewing the outer curve to the far end of the seam allowance. Knot the thread and cut, leaving a ¼-inch tail.

If you reach the far end of the strip and find that it is not long enough to extend into the flower area, you will have to pull it off and start over. What happened? The patch was marked using the template, so it had to be long enough to begin with—if you remembered to leave ¼-inch seam allowances when cutting. The answer is in how the fabric was shifted with the needle. Instead of moving the fabric directly over to the mas-

Fig. 7-25 Start the running stitch in the end seam allowance.

Fig. 7-26 Working only ⅓ inch ahead of the running stitch, shift the stem over to the penciled line.

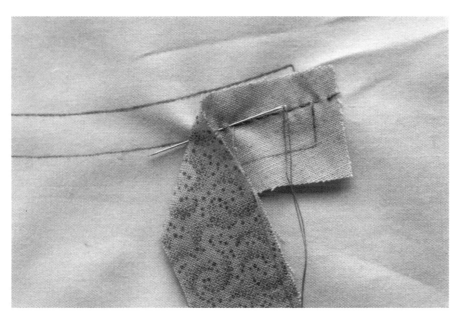

Fig. 7-27 Fold the stem back on itself with the needle still in the fabric to see if you are on the master line. If not, pull the needle out, align the fabric and restitch.

Fig. 7-28 If the stem is rippled after the inside curve is appliqued, the stem patch was shifted too much when sewing the first side. Undo and try again.

Fig. 7-29 Trim the sewn seam allowance to about ⅛ inch before folding the stem over and stitching down.

ter line, it was moved, however slightly, back toward the seam already sewn. This results in a very wavy stem when the final edge is sewn down (Fig. 7–28). It will take some practice to sew this seam properly, but after appliqueing several stems you will be quite proficient.

If the seam allowance on the sewn edge is too wide, trim it now (Fig. 7 29). Next fold the stem fabric over so that the fabric is right side up. It should be smooth and flat. The inside curved edge is to be sewn using the applique technique discussed in Figs. 7–8 and 7–9. Trim the seam allowance, if necessary, as you sew. Each edge has been sewn using a different method, but the finished product should look smooth and neat.

Circles

Unless a circle is quite large, say 3 inches in diameter, it is very difficult to make it really round, even following a master pattern. I finally decided not to use master patterns for small circles, but to applique them in the following manner.

Using a pencil, trace around a circle template on the applique fabric. Cut the patch out on the penciled line (seam allowance included). With a knotted, single thread, sew a tiny running stitch around the entire outer edge of the patch. The stitches should be as close to the edge as possible without fraying the material. Draw the thread up as tight as possible to gather the fabric. *Do not* cut the thread. The patch will look like a ball. Flatten the ball so that it forms a circle with

Fig. 7-30 Making a circle. Trace a circle template (seams included) and cut the patch out on the penciled line. With a single, knotted thread, sew a tiny running stitch around the entire outer edge. Draw the thread up as tightly as possible. The circle forms a ball. Flatten into a circle and even the gathers with the needle's tip. Don't knot or cut the thread.

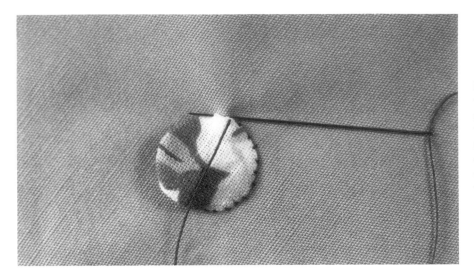

Fig. 7-31 Use the gathering thread and applique with small stitches around the circle's edge to get a smooth curve. There may be small points around the circle. Take a stitch into a point and it will disappear when the thread is pulled taut.

the raw edges centered on the wrong side (Fig. 7–30). Position the circle in the desired area and applique down, using the same thread that gathered the circle. The applique stitches should be very close together (Fig. 7–31). If any little points have formed, take a stitch right into the point and it will disappear when the thread is pulled taut.

A circle can be stuffed, if you desire. Sew as directed above, but after sewing two-thirds of the circle, poke a little loose batting into the opening and then continue appliqueing. Don't stuff too tightly or the background fabric will pull out of shape.

It will probably take several tries to determine the correct size of the template, since so much of the fabric is drawn up to the back when gathering. A variety of small items can be used for circle templates, for example: the end of a thread spool, various sized coins, and small bottles.

ORCHARD RIBBONS

Like Victorian Wicker, Orchard Ribbons is not beginner's applique, but I have my beginners learn with it. Applique will never be a problem for you, if you master both of these blocks. I would suggest doing the Victorian Wicker first, since it is easier (see color Figs. 1 and 3).

Start by appliqueing the center "U" shapes (7–33A), but not the circles (7–33B). They are appliqued last. Start the "U" on a long outer side and work toward the inner curved hook. Clip only just in front of where you are working. The depth of the curves will require narrow seam allowances and close clipping. Use care not to clip into the seam allowance and

take *tiny* stitches. The outer curved ribbons are appliqued next. First, applique 7–33C and 7–33D. The edges that are covered by 7–33E and 7–33F are not turned under. Hold those portions down with running stitches in the seam allowances. 7–33E is appliqued next, then 7–33F. Remember, to trace the reverse patches (C-R, D-R, E-R, F-R) onto the applique fabric, the template must be turned over. The circles are done in the manner described above (Circles).

Again, don't expect perfect results to begin with. Each applique will look progressively better as you practice. I do recommend appliqueing all of one type of patch before going on to the next. In that way, you get a lot of practice with a particular shape.

Additional Thoughts on Applique

The blocks covered in this chapter are not beginner's designs! They are advanced applique, taught with a completely new method. If you are like all my other students, you are now exhausted and very frustrated. And you've probably produced less than spectacular results. You are undoubtedly wondering why I chose these patterns and not something easier. After all you are a beginner—at least to the master pattern technique.

I could certainly show you to how to applique an easy design like Sunbonnet Sue. That pattern has no really difficult points and only very gentle curves. But would I really be helping you? You need to learn how to do the difficult applique. I imagine you can figure out easy applique for yourself. As I tell my classroom students, "Yes, applique is hard for a beginner new to this technique. Yes, it does take time to learn, but once you have learned how to handle the needle and manipulate fabric, applique is exciting, creative and rewarding.

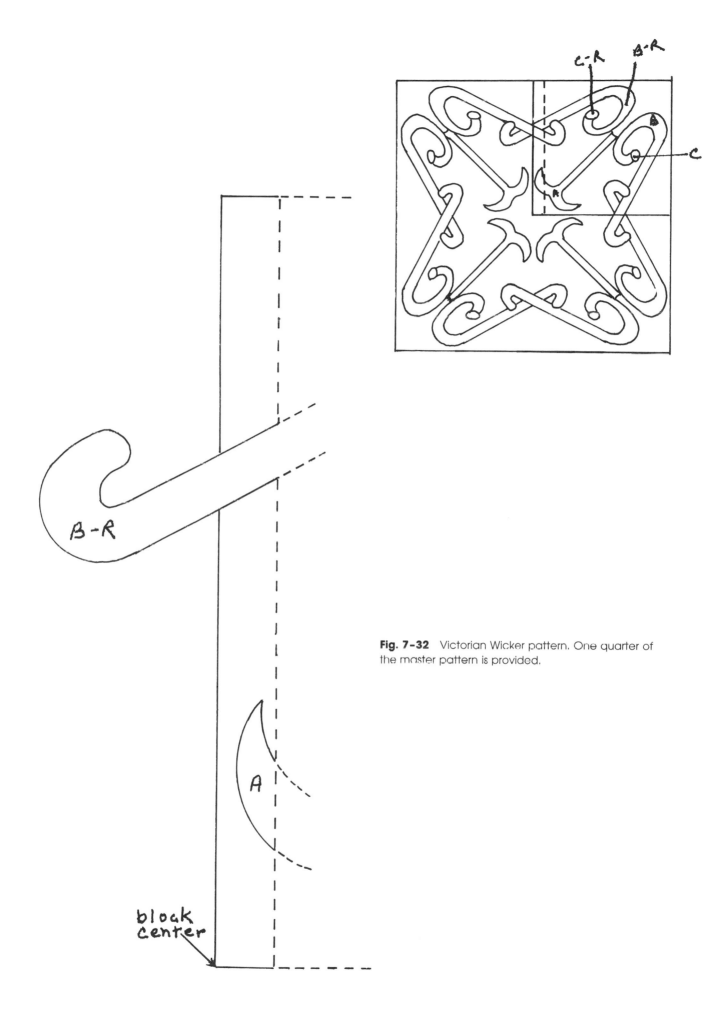

Fig. 7-32 Victorian Wicker pattern. One quarter of the master pattern is provided.

Fig. 7-32 *continued*

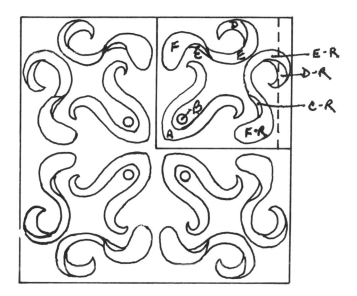

Fig. 7-33 Orchard Ribbons pattern. One quarter of the master pattern is provided.

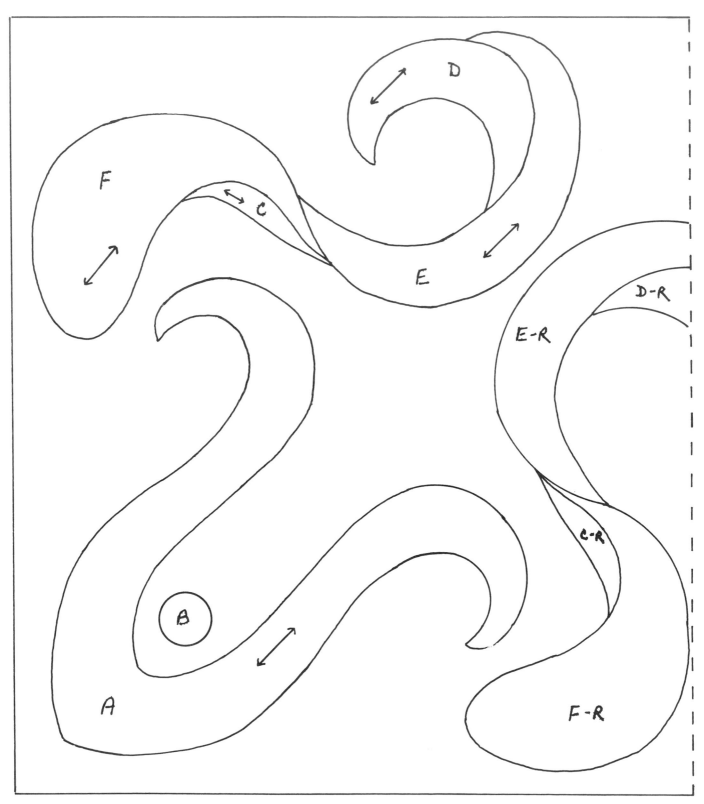

Fig. 7-33 *continued*

Chapter Eight

Piecing and Assembling Difficult Shapes

As with all the piecing discussed, marking and sewing is exactly the same for curves and stars, but there are logistical problems resulting from the shapes of the patches. These particular problems will be covered in this chapter.

PIECING CURVES: SPINNING COMET

No matter how gentle or sharp the curve, the trick is *not* to pin the entire seam allowance at the same time. In this instance, I will use the Spinning Comet block (color Fig. 4) as an example. I developed this design to give extensive experience with curves, both gentle and acute. The more gentle curves will probably not present any problems, but do follow the directions given below for all curves. The piecing will be easier and the pieces will lie flat when completed.

Pressing Curved Blocks

Before beginning to piece Spinning Comet, review the instructions in Chapter 5 on pressing. With that information in mind, use great care when pressing any small curved units, since they will stretch with very little pressure. Some curved seam allowances will fold more readily to one side. Which way should they go? There is no hard and fast rule. Check the right side of the block and finger press the seams to see which direction looks better. In some instances, the direction patch seam allowances lie may have to be changed in mid-patch. Trying to decide how best to press seam allowances can be more of a challenge than piecing a complicated block.

Premarking Your Own Curved Templates

On each of the template patterns in Spinning Comet, slash lines have been given for matching to a corresponding slash mark. If you are working with another

Fig. 8-1 Mark slash lines in the seam allowances corresponding to the marks on the template patterns. These lines must meet when sewn together.

pattern, you will have to make your own. Take the two working templates that must be joined and fit them together. Mark slash lines from one template to the other at the height of the curve (center) and in as many places as you think necessary. Transfer these lines into the seam allowance of the fabric patches when marking, prior to cutting. It doesn't matter if the slash marks do not divide the curve exactly. What is important is to join the concave and convex curves at the corresponding markings. Also transfer the "X" marks which designate the beginning or ending of a patch.

Spinning Comet Assembly

The instructions for piecing the most acute curve (A to B) are given first. Follow these directions exactly for piecing all curves in Spinning Comet.

Pattern template A (Fig. 8–5) is almost a 180-degree curve, or a lopsided half circle, that fits into template B. Both of these templates are marked with slash lines. These lines should be placed on your working templates and then duplicated onto the fabric patches in the seam allowance area (Fig. 8–1). After marking the slash lines and cutting out patch B, clip halfway into the seam allowance on the concave

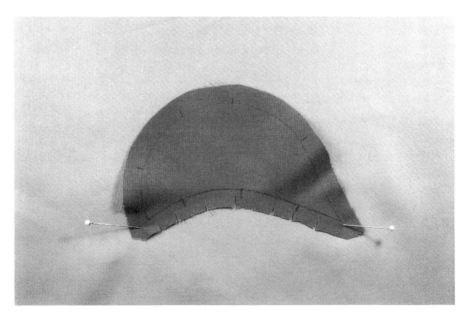

Fig. 8-2 Clip the concave edge of patch C at one-inch intervals and clip one-half the distance to the penciled line.

Fig. 8-3 Pin at the center mark and the beginning corner. Also match the marks and pin. Sew from the corner to the center.

edge every inch (Fig. 8–2). This allows the curved edge to be pulled into a fairly straight line. It is not necessary to clip patch A, but you may find it helpful to cut tiny V shapes from its convex edge to remove excess material that would wrinkle if you decided to press the seam allowance over on itself.

Pin only one-half of the seam allowance to begin with. Match the center markings and each successive mark, down to the point where you will start sewing (Fig. 8–3). Match the X's on each patch or they will never fit together.

Start sewing the seam allowance, as usual. When working with curves, it will be more difficult to align the penciled stitching lines on both patches, but it is essential that you do so. You will probably find that only two or three stitches at a time can be taken on the needle (on a straight seam, four or five can be taken). Once you have sewn up to the center pin, stop sewing and pin the remainder of the seam line, matching slash marks. Finish sewing the seam line (Fig. 8–4).

This block is joined in quarter units and assembled from the center out (Fig. 8–6). Each quarter unit is joined in the same manner and pinned and pieced as just described. Piece A and B together. Join C to B–A, making sure that the long point of C starts at the X mark on B or the seam lines will not fit. Next, D is

Fig. 8-4 Pin the remaining marks and corner, and sew to the corner. Knot and end as usual.

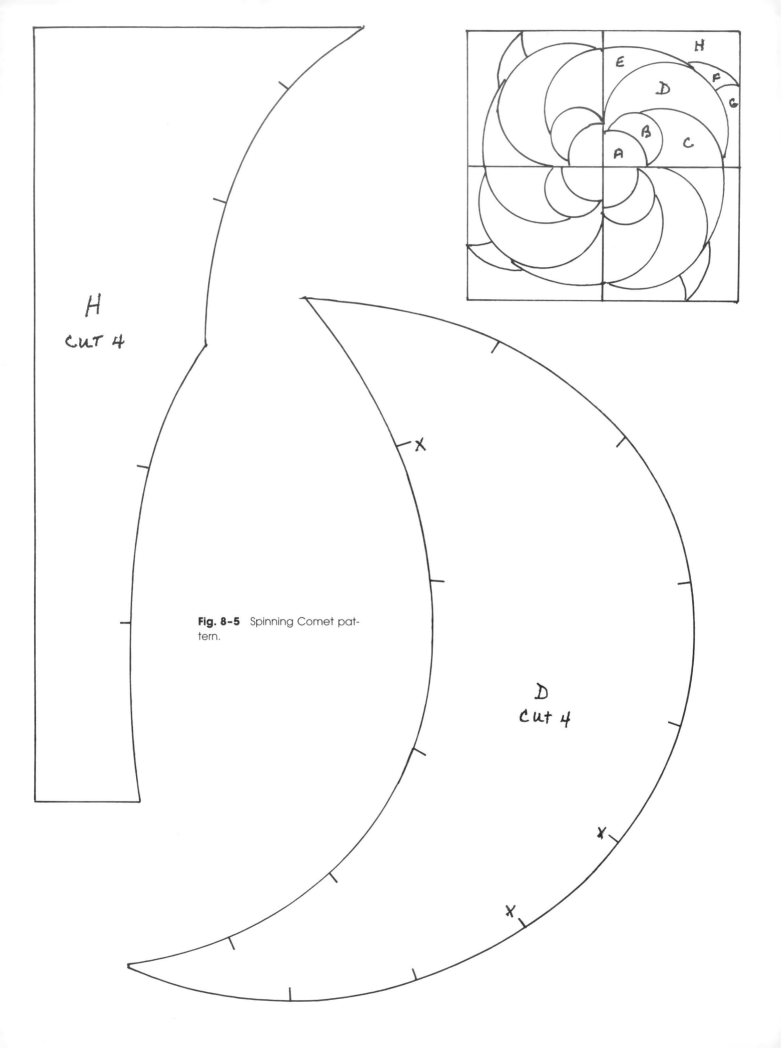

Fig. 8-5 Spinning Comet pattern.

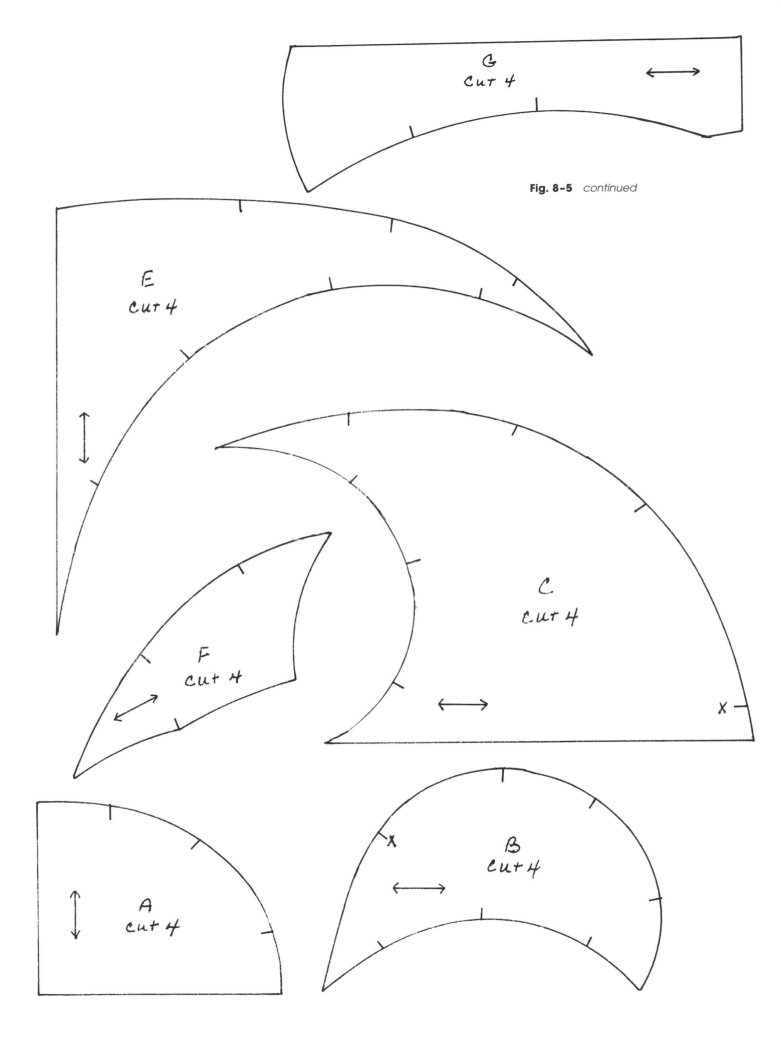

G
Cut 4

Fig. 8-5 *continued*

E
cut 4

C
cut 4

F
cut 4

A
cut 4

B
cut 4

Step 1

Step 2

Step 3

Step 4

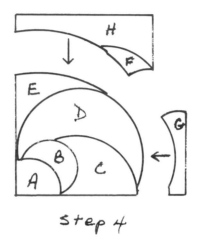

Fig. 8-6 Spinning Comet assembly.

joined to the B–C edges, matching the X's. Join E to the D side of the full unit, again matching the X on the convex side of D.

Join F to H, then piece this F–H unit to the convex edge of the larger unit along the E–D edge, matching X's. G is the final patch. Join the short, curved edge of G to F, then flop G over (see Chapter 5, Joining Multiple Edges—Flopping) and sew its long edge to the D–C edge, matching X's. One quarter of the block is pieced. Repeat for the remaining three quarter units. *Note: Not all patches will met at the quarter seam lines of Spinning Comet. It is an asymmetrical block.*

Join two quarter units together starting at A and sewing to the outer edges. One half of the block is completed. At this point, most quilters would join the remaining two quarter units together and then sew the two halves together with one long seam to complete the block. There usually is a problem with this final joining of two half blocks: accuracy in the center.

To have absolute matching in the block's center, it is imperative to *always* sew from the center patch out. To do this with large quarter blocks is easy. First, sew two quarters together from the center patch to the outer edge. Add the third quarter starting at A in Spinning Comet (the center) and sewing to the outer edge; three-quarters of the block are now joined. The final block is flopped in as detailed in Chapter 5, Joining Multiple Edges, with the following exceptions: the seaming is started at the center patch and goes to the outside edge, and two threads are used instead of a single one.

PIECING STARS: HORIZON STAR, COSMIC LIGHT, BEACON FIRE

Any time six or more patches are joined together, you are working with the fundamentals of joining a star center, even though the finished design may not form a full star. Each quilter has an opinion on how best to

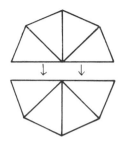

piece a star and have an accurate center joining. I believe the majority join an eight-pointed star first in units of two, then four, and finally the two sets of four together with a straight seam to form the full star (Fig. 8–7). I have trouble with this method. Slight shifting seems to result, at least for me, and the center isn't always perfect. When piecing a twelve-pointed star this problem is really mangified. I have found the following method very easy for beginners and extremely accurate. We will work with the Horizon Star block (see color Fig. 5).

Fig. 8-7 The method generally used for piecing a star. The unit is joined in quarters, then halves, and finally into a completed block.

Fig. 8-8 Join patches in a row and stitch from the center to the outside edge for absolute accuracy.

Fig. 8-9 There will be a small hole at the very center of the star when the final seam is sewn. If the hole is large enough to put your finger in, something went wrong while marking or piecing. Try again!

Fig. 8-10 The hole must be closed. Bring the needle up from the back of the block into a patch at the edge of the hole.

Horizon Star Assembly

You will notice that the edges of the templates are marked with varying numbers of slash marks (Fig. 8–14). These do not have to be sewn slash to slash as with the curved patches in Spinning Comet. They simply indicate which patch edge joins to its neighbor patch. For instance, the single slash on patch A joins to the edge of patch C that has a single slash.

To piece the center, pin patch A to patch B and sew the seam from the center point to the outer edge. This is important since shifting of even a single thread or

two at the point would throw the center matching off. It is not as crucial at the outer edge. Again, careful marking, pinning and sewing are mandatory for accuracy.

Continue adding A and B patches alternately until all patches are sewn into a single row (Fig. 8–8). Close the star by sewing the end patches A and B together. This method of joining will leave a small hole in the very center of the star (Fig. 8–9). If the hole is large enough for you to stick your finger through, something went wrong. Was the template marking

Fig. 8-11 Pick up a few threads at the very point of each patch around the edge of the hole in order of piecing.

Fig. 8-12 Pull the thread taut from the right side of the block. The hole will close tightly.

really accurate at the points? Did you sew on the pencil lines or go off a bit? Did you sew from the center of the star to the outside edges? Decide where you went wrong, rip out and make the necessary corrections.

Closing the Center Hole

The hole must now be closed. Be sure to use a single, knotted thread that best matches all the fabrics. Bring the needle up through the fabric from the under side of the block into one patch at the edge of the hole (Fig.

8-10). All remaining stitching will be done from the *right* side of the block. Take a tiny stitch into the very point of each one of the patches at the hole's edge (Fig. 8-11). When all patches have been so stitched, pull the thread taut (Fig. 8-12). The hole should close with the center matching very accurately. If it is slightly off, take a few tiny stitches across the center to draw the unaligned points together (Fig. 8-13). When pulled taut, these stitches should not be visible. Take the needle to the back of the block, knot and then cut the thread. A perfect center!

Fig. 8-13 If the patch points do not align, take a few stitches across the center to pull the unaligned points together. Take the thread to the back of the block, knot and cut.

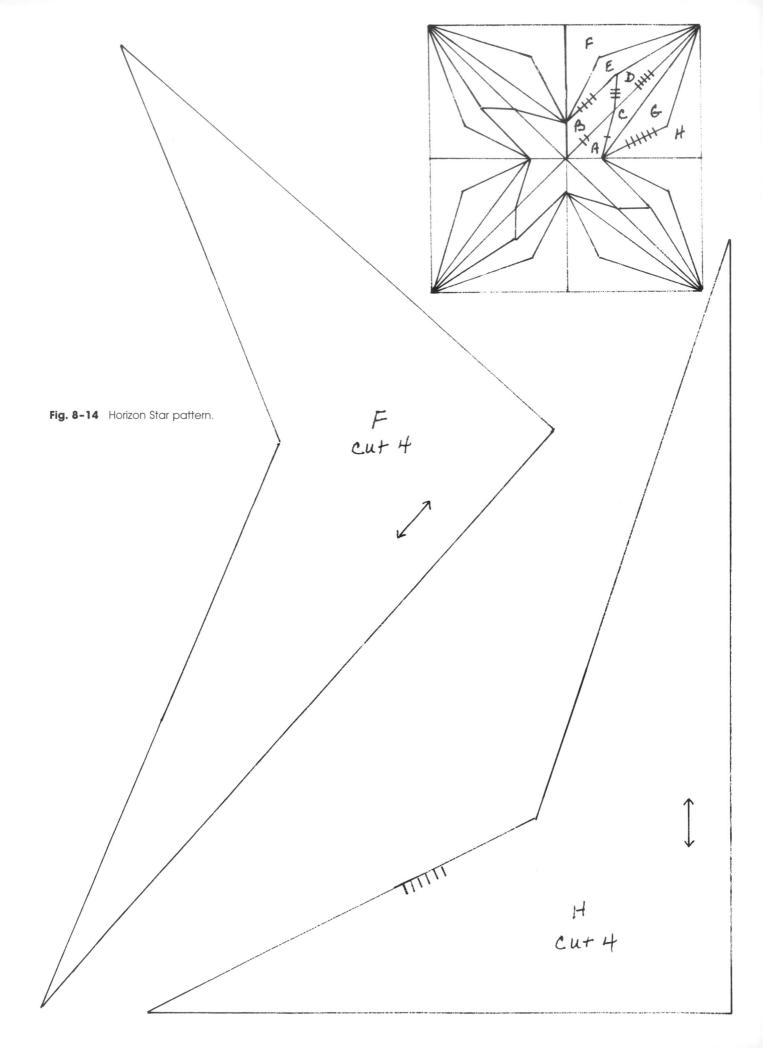

Fig. 8-14 Horizon Star pattern.

F
cut 4

H
cut 4

Fig. 8-14 *continued*

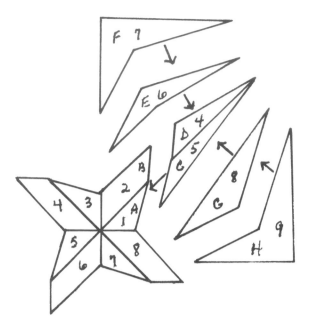

Fig. 8-15 Horizon Star assembly.

The remainder of the block is joined as in Figure 8-15. Join patches C and D together on the five slash side. Then to D add patches E, then F. To C add G, then H. Repeat this three more times. You now have four quarter units that are each joined to the center star by flopping them with one continuous seam.

Cosmic Light Assembly
Cosmic Light is a pieced design (Fig. 8-16) that is to be appliqued to a background block as Miner's Lamp was. Study patch 8-16B; it can be cut either as a single shape or as two patches, which could be of either the same fabric (sometimes a piecing seam gives added design detail) or two different fabrics. Also note that the line on the side edge of B is to be matched to the line in patch C when piecing.

The assembly (Fig. 8-17) is not difficult, but do pin both edges and the center of 8-16E to 8-16CD before sewing. Press, then baste the raw edges under as directed in Chapter 5: Basting. Center and pin the pieced block onto the background block. Applique in place. Patch 8-16F has been provided if you want the entire block pieced. In that case, appliqueing to a background block is not necessary.

Beacon Fire Assembly
At first glance, Beacon Fire does not appear to present any special problems, but look more closely at the patterns (Fig. 8-19). It is comprised of triangles each of which appear to have at least two equal sides. Wrong. Most of the triangle sides are not of the same length, so great care must be taken to match the proper patch sides together. Again, make use of the slash marks on the template patterns as you did for Horizon Star.

Beacon Fire assembly is not difficult piecing, but follow the assembly in Figure 8-18 very closely, making sure that appropriate marks are in the seam allowance when cutting out the patches. These lines are not matched as in Figure 8-16, but indicate which patch edges are to be joined. Complete the block and press as before.

ADDITIONAL PATTERNS: JEWELED SUN, TWISTED BANDS, FRAGMENTED STAR

Jeweled Sun (Fig. 8-20), Twisted Bands (Fig. 8-21), and Fragmented Star (Fig. 8-22) patterns are given at the conclusion of this chapter. See Fig. 6-5 for Twisted Bands' assembly. No detailed assembly instructions are provided for Jeweled Sun or Fragmented Star. At this point, you should be accomplished enough to decide upon the best method.

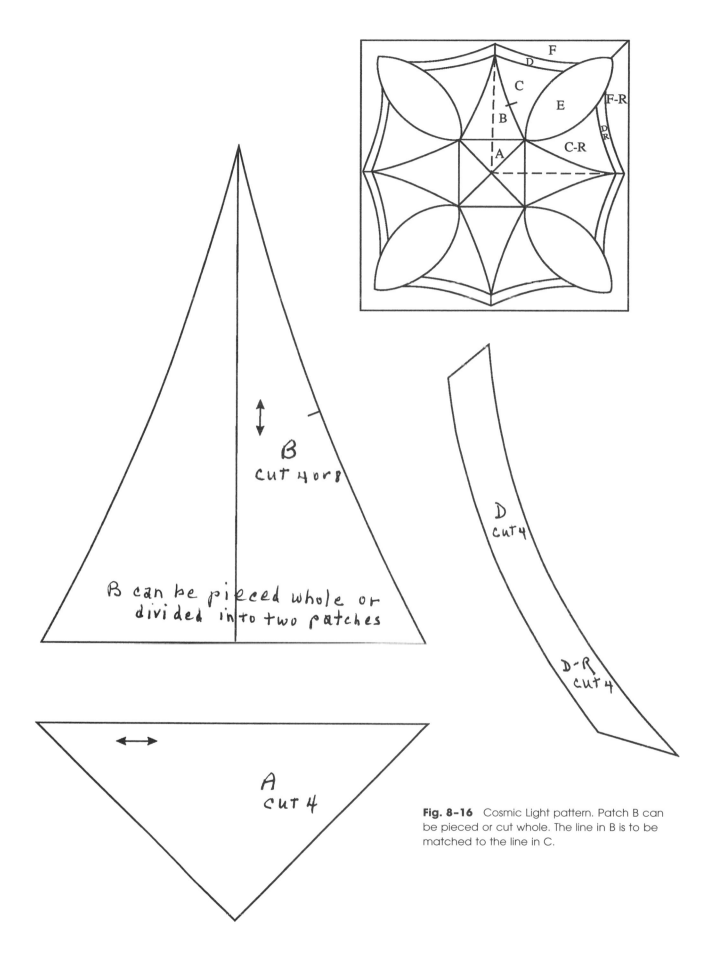

B
cut 4 or 8

B can be pieced whole or divided into two patches

A
cut 4

D
cut 4

D-R
cut 4

Fig. 8-16 Cosmic Light pattern. Patch B can be pieced or cut whole. The line in B is to be matched to the line in C.

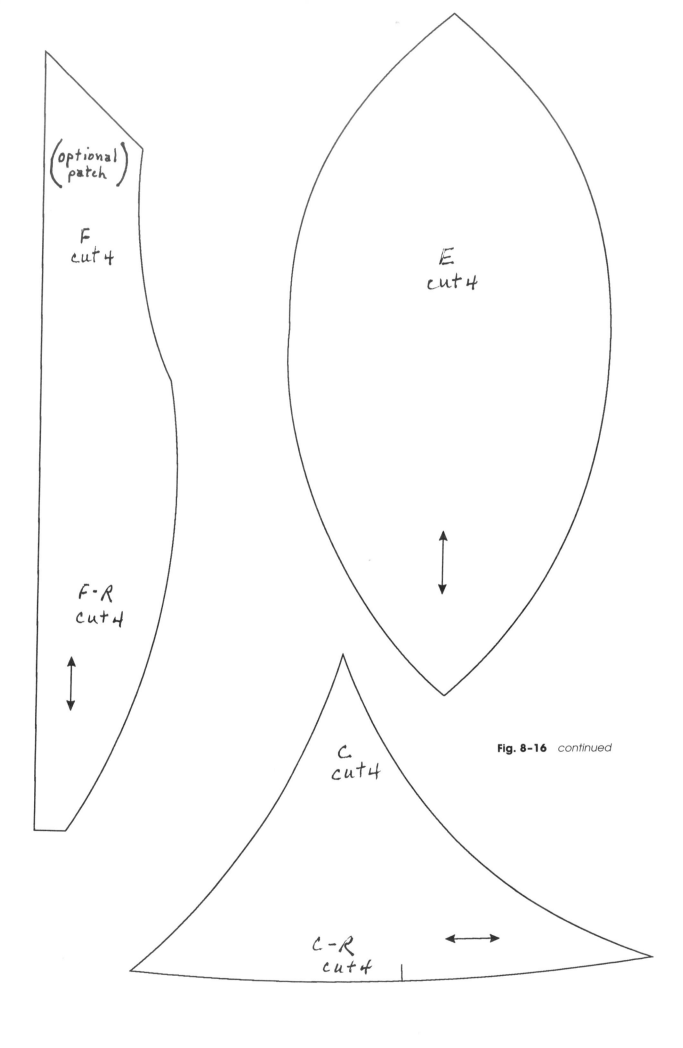

(optional) patch

F cut 4

F-R cut 4

E cut 4

C cut 4

C-R cut 4

Fig. 8-16 *continued*

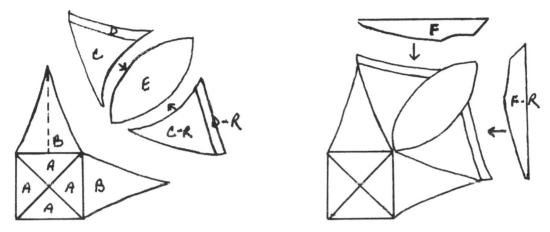

Fig. 8-17 Cosmic Light assembly. This block can be appliqued to a background block or totally pieced. In that instance, patch F will be used to create the outside edge of the block.

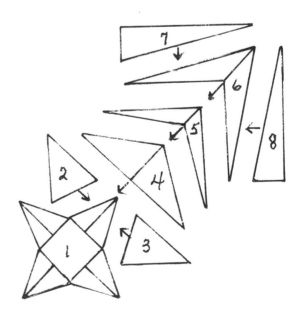

Fig. 8-18 Beacon Fire assembly.

Fig. 8-19 Beacon Fire pattern.

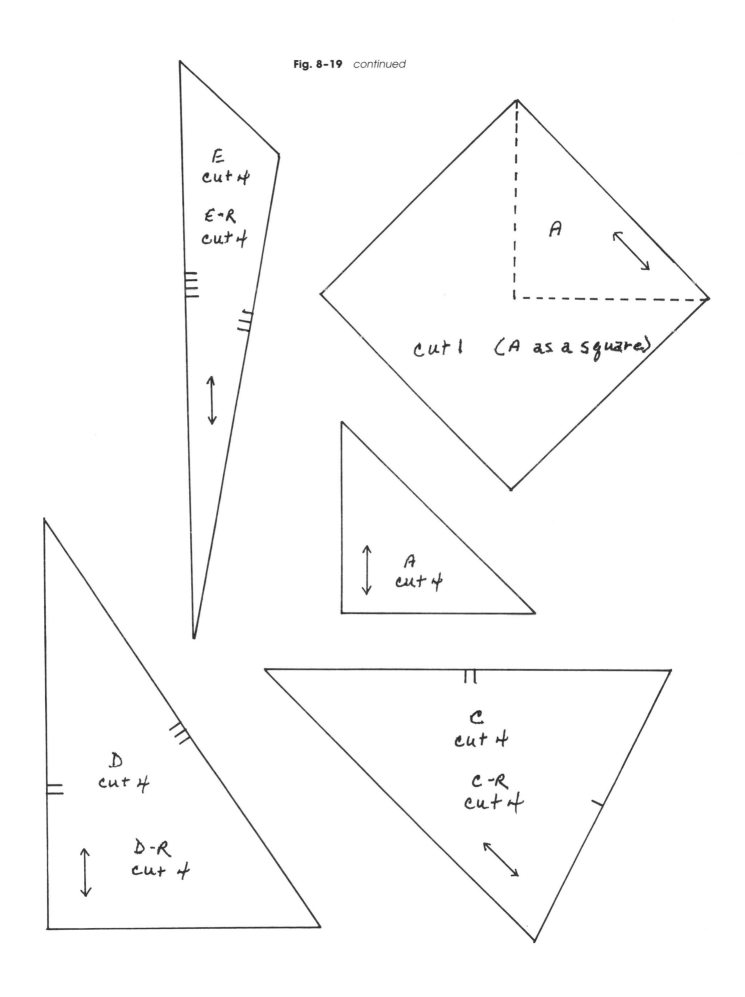

Fig. 8-19 *continued*

E
cut 4

E-R
cut 4

A

cut 1 (A as a square)

A
cut 4

D
cut 4

D-R
cut 4

C
cut 4

C-R
cut 4

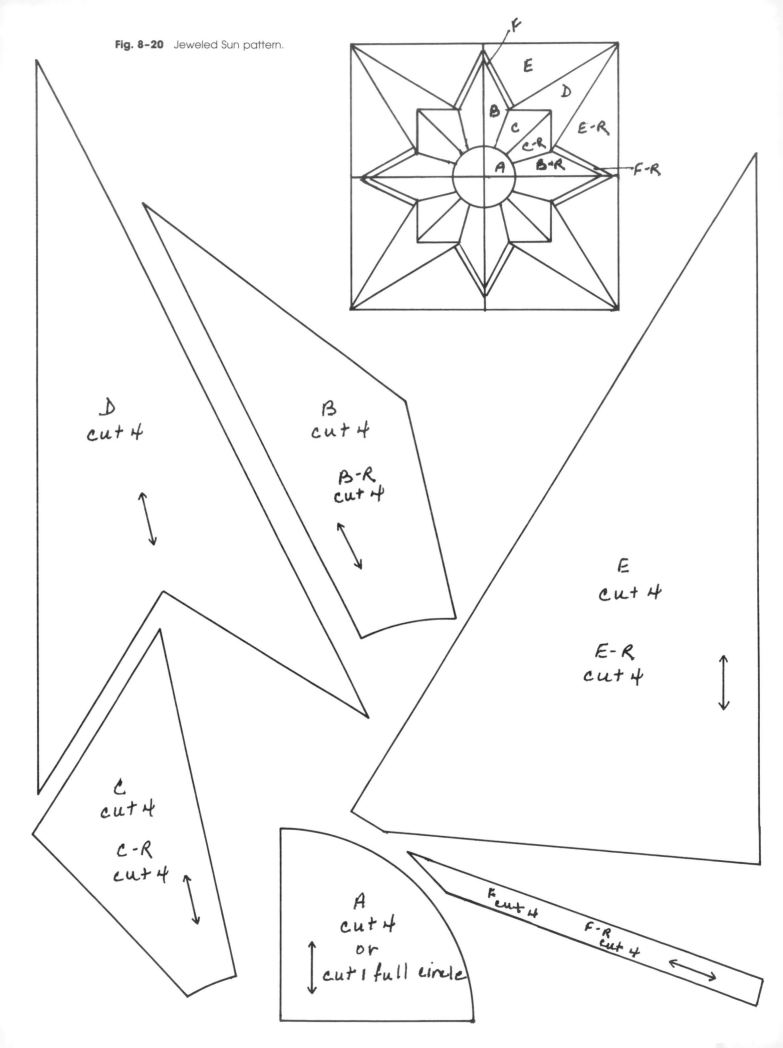

Fig. 8-20 Jeweled Sun pattern.

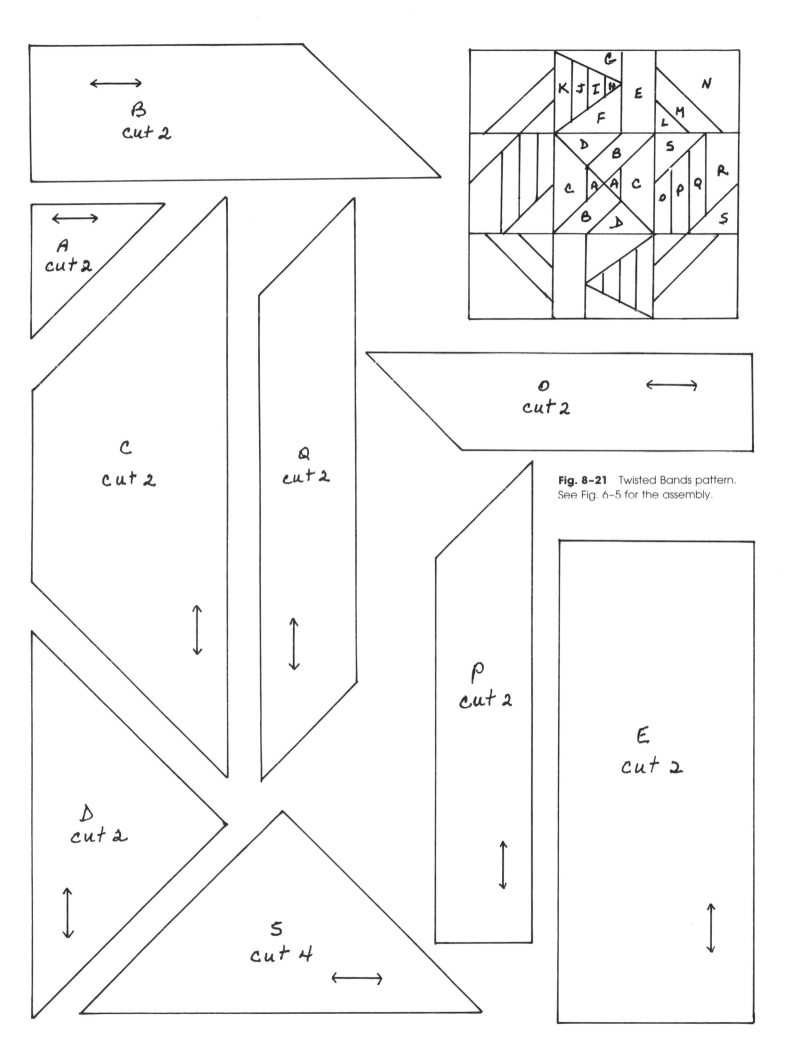

B
cut 2

A
cut 2

C
cut 2

D
cut 2

Q
cut 2

S
cut 4

O
cut 2

P
cut 2

E
cut 2

Fig. 8-21 Twisted Bands pattern.
See Fig. 6-5 for the assembly.

Fig. 8-21 *continued*

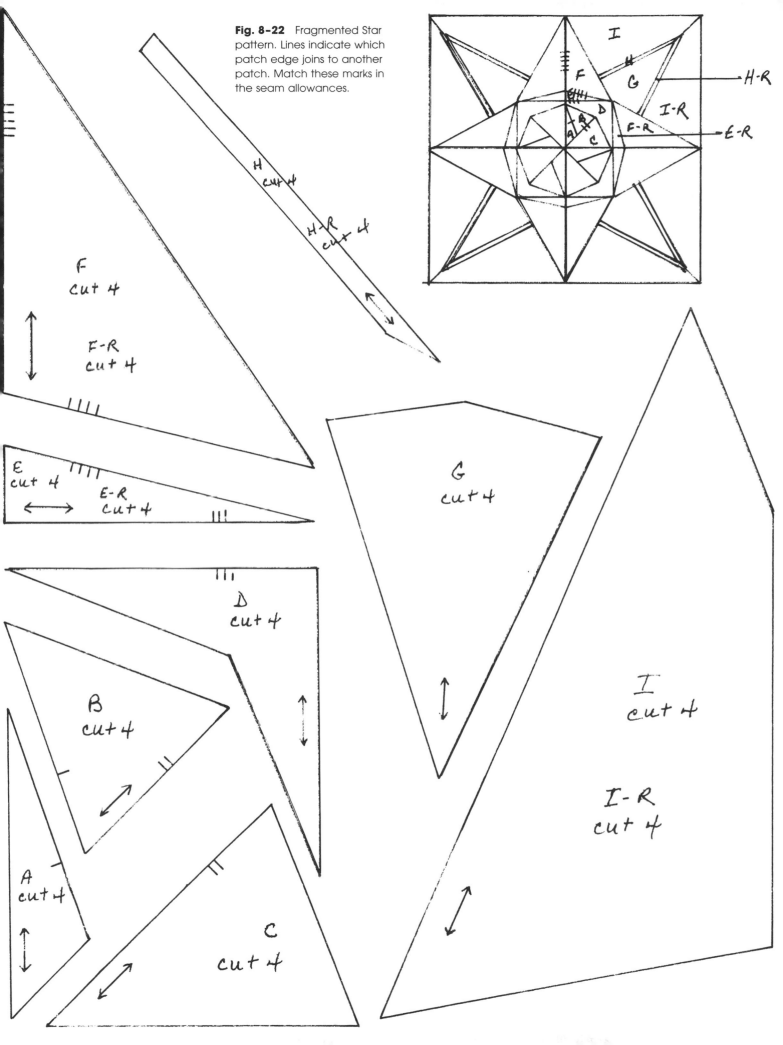

Fig. 8-22 Fragmented Star pattern. Lines indicate which patch edge joins to another patch. Match these marks in the seam allowances.

Chapter Nine

Strip Assembly

All the techniques for piecing and applique have been discussed thoroughly. After you have constructed all the blocks needed for the quilt, you are ready to set them together with the sashing that has been marked and cut (see Chapter 4). Lay all the blocks on the floor and arrange them so that you are pleased with the balance. The blocks should be placed so that the colors and patterns are evenly distributed. For instance, if you have two blocks that are appliqued and contain a lot of red, don't put them next to each other. There are some pleasing arrangements shown in the color plates. Please realize, however, that no single arrangement is necessarily right; your choice should be dictated by both design and color use. Once you have decided on the placement, make a notation of it on your quilt layout, so you can refer to it later when setting the blocks.

MARKING QUILTING PATTERNS

Before the strip is basted together, it must be marked for the quilting pattern you intend to use. A pieced block, such as Beacon Fire, can be outline quilted ¼ to ⅓ inch inside the seams. Outline quilting is marked *after* the strip has been basted together and set in the frame, and you are actually quilting that area.

A second quilting method follows an appliqued

design. The lines are marked, freehand, after the strip has been basted and set in the frame. It is almost the same as with the pieced block, but instead of following a geometric shape and using a ruler as a guide, you follow a free-form design and do the marking without a ruler. These lines are placed the same distance from the appliqued design as the outline quilting lines are from the seams, i.e., ¼ to ⅓ inch from the applique edge.

A third quilting method is a free-form, fancy pattern in either blocks, sashing, or borders (See Fig. 9–6). It does not have to follow a pieced or appliqued shape already in the block. The pattern must be put on the fabric *before* the strip is basted together. For sashing and borders, I would do this before they are sewn to the blocks. The design is handled and applied as a master pattern (see Chapter 7, Master Pattern Applique).

A fourth method can be produced by using a moveable template. The shape is usually fairly simple, for it must be cut out with scissors from Mylar or a manila folder. Again, the strip should be in the frame and ready to quilt. After placing the template on the surface of the material, use a sharp pencil to trace the design onto the fabric. You can make your own quilt template, or you can purchase machine-made stencils. The ready-made stencils are usually fairly expensive, however, and may not be very accurate. If you are going to use an elaborate quilting design, I would recommend that the master pattern technique be used, both from the standpoint of accuracy and cost.

For the sampler quilt used as the example project, you will be using all four quilting methods. Fancy designs will be used in the borders, sashing, and the open areas of blocks such as Miner's Lamp. The designs in this chapter, Figs. 9–6 to 9–8, will give you some idea of what can be done.

Make master patterns for these designs. The entire quilt layout (Fig. 9–6) is keyed to the quilting designs shown in Figures 9–7 and 9–8. The border and sashing patterns should be put on heavier paper the finished size and length of a repeat. For example, the

block is 16 inches and the sashing is 4 inches wide. Cut a paper template 20 inches long and 4 inches wide to extend the length of one block and the sashing intersection. Transfer Figures 9–7a and 9–7b for the quilting pattern.

SETTING BLOCKS TO SASHING

Piecing sashing to blocks is done exactly the same as joining small patches, except that you are constructing larger units. You do have to be careful that the sash is pinned in evenly. Match the corner pencil lines and, using your finger, crease the center of the sash on its longest edge. Pin this crease mark to the seam line at the center of the block. Then pin each corner and any additional locations necessary to hold it securely (Fig. 9–1). Sew as usual. Remember, *do not sew* into the seam allowances.

Fig. 9-1 Find the sash center and pin it to the center of the block's edge. Any long units should be creased and pinned in this manner to insure accurate piecing. Always pin on the pencil lines.

Fig. 9-2 Completed top strips for twin to floor quilt. Strips 1 and 2 are the blocks and sashing. Strips 3 through 6 are the borders. The patterned areas indicate fabric extensions to square off the strip ends.

Twin to Floor Strip Units

For the twin to the floor layout, you will have strip 1, with three blocks, each separated by a sash. Strip 2 has three blocks, each separated by a sash, plus the long center sash down one edge. There will be four border units, each comprised of the inner border and outer border. This makes a total of six strip units that have to be quilted and then joined together to make the quilt (Fig. 9–2).

CUTTING THE BATT AND BACKING

The backing fabric and batt must now be cut for each of the strips in Fig. 9–2. Use the completed top strips as patterns. Lay strip 1 on the backing fabric and cut around its raw edges. Do the same thing for the batt, making sure that the batt has first been separated into a single layer. (Some batts tend to stick together after being packaged for a period of time). Repeat this cutting process for each of the strips in Fig. 9–2. Because you have cut around the outer edges of the strips, the seam allowances have automatically been included in the backing and batt.

All of the backing strips can be cut down the length of the fabric as in cutting method 1 (see Chapter 4). You will use 41 inches of the 44-inch wide material. For some quilts, cutting method 2 might be the most economical. Again, you would piece the fabric where necessary and treat the seam as if it didn't exist.

STRIP ASSEMBLY

Place the backing strip, wrong side up, on a table. Place the batt strip on top of it. Smooth out any wrinkles in the batt. Carefully lay the top strip on the batt, right side up (Fig. 9–3). Make sure that any loose threads have been trimmed from the seams of the strip. Pin the three units (backing, batt, and top) together at the outer edges (Fig. 9–4).

The strip must be basted together through all three layers. Use a "sharp" or embroidery needle and a long thread. Basting thread works well and is certainly cheaper than #50 thread. In any case, use only white thread; colored thread can leave dots of color in the fabric when it's removed.

Fig. 9-3 Assembling the backing, batt, and top. Make sure all loose threads have been trimmed away and wrinkles pressed out.

Fig. 9-4 The strip is pinned together and ready for basting.

The basting stitches can be about 2 inches long. The basting rows should be 2 inches apart and 12 inches in from each end of the strip. In the middle area of the strip, the rows can be 4 inches apart. Work the basting rows up the strip in a serpentine fashion. This method will hold the strip securely (Fig. 9–5).

Fig. 9-5 Top view of the strip basted together. The basting rows must be no more than 2 inches apart for a distance of 12 inches at each end of the strip; otherwise, you will have difficulty when quilting that area.

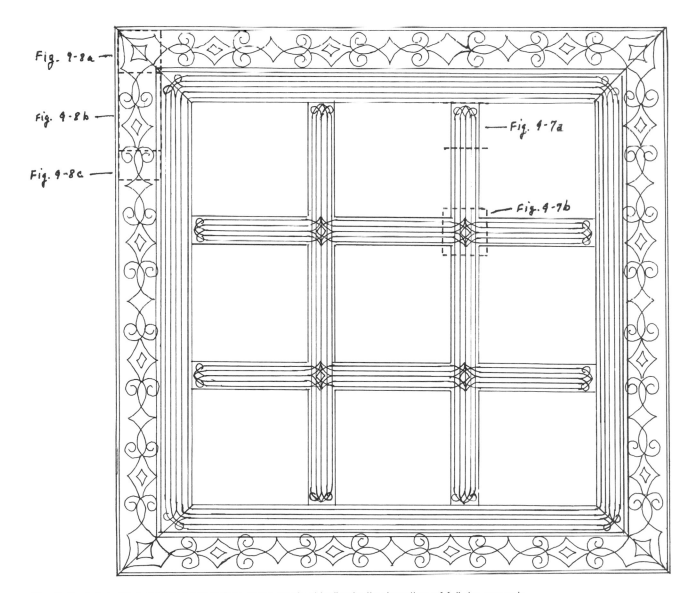

Fig. 9-6 Full quilting design layout. The areas marked indicate the location of full-size repeats.

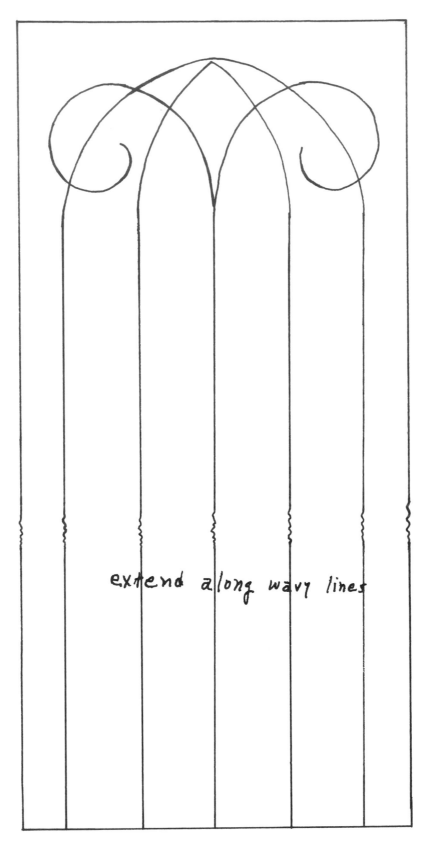

extend along wavy lines

Fig. 9-7a Sashing end pattern. Extend the master pattern lines to the needed length.

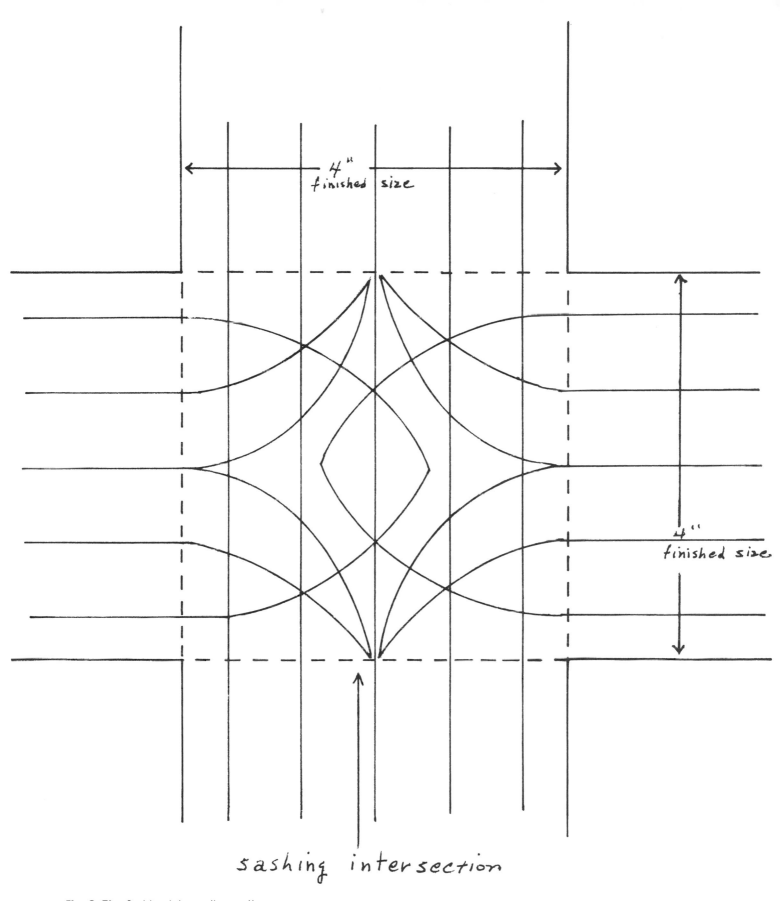

Fig. 9-7b Sashing intersection pattern.

Line A

narrow
inner
border

Fig. 9-8a Outer border corner. The narrow inner border is pieced to the outer border and then both are treated as a single fabric when the quilting pattern is applied. Note that line A is only used at the corner turning.

Fig. 9-8b Outer border main repeat. Note that line B is used only on the inner repeats, not at the corner turning.

← line B

9-8c joining line →

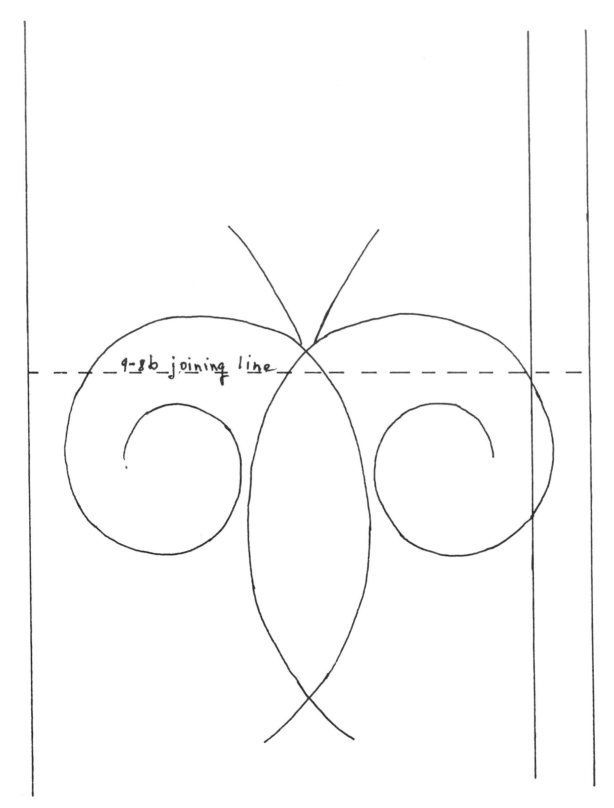

Fig. 9-8c   Join to Fig. 9–8b at the dash line for the entire repeat pattern.

Chapter Ten

Quilting As You Go

The strip is now ready to be pinned into the quilt-as-you-go frame. A major advantage in this type of quilt making is that you can be quilting on a strip while you are still piecing blocks for it. This not only seems to speed up the process, but it keeps you from being bored by having to do all of one phase before going on to the next.

The frame you use can be a purchased needlepoint frame or one that has been made by following the directions in Chapter 1. I have frames in varying lengths from 12 inches, for borders or small pillows, to 36 inches, a really cumbersome size. The most versatile, easily handled frame length is 24 inches. This length will allow you to quilt a 16-inch block with an attached 5- or 6-inch wide sashing.

ATTACHING THE STRIP TO THE FRAME

Place the shortest edge of the basted strip, top up, along the edge of the tape. The loose edge of the tape should be toward the center of the frame (see Fig. 1–2e). Make sure that the strip is centered on the tape. Pin the seam allowance of the strip to the edge of

the tape about every 2 inches (Fig. 10–1). Do not pin too close to the dowel or you may quilt the tape to the strip (Fig. 10–2). *Note:* If you live in an area of high humidity, do not use pins. Baste the strip to the tape with white thread to prevent rust spots. Also, protect the tack heads or staples used to attach the tape to the dowel by painting them with clear nail polish. Let the polish dry thoroughly before using the frame.

It is easiest to pin or baste one end of the strip into the frame, roll half the strip around the dowel, then pin or baste the opposite end of the strip to the other tape and roll that end.

When rolling the strip onto the dowel, you must take care to roll the basted unit as one piece. Even though it has been basted, it can shift easily. Don't tug on the strip as it is rolled. Grasp the fabric strip gently, but firmly, making sure it goes around the dowel as a single unit. Each dowel should be rotated to the outside of the frame so that the basted unit lies above the dowels (see Fig. 1–2e).

As you roll the strip onto the dowel, the backing will be going around a smaller circumference than the top because of the batt's thickness. Therefore, the backing will wrinkle as the strip is rolled on (Fig.

Fig. 10-1 Basting the quilt into the quilt-as-you-go frame.

Fig. 10-2 Back view of the tape. Baste or pin close to the edge of the tape.

Fig. 10-3 End view of the basted unit that has been rolled onto the frame. The end bar is removed. Notice the wrinkling of the strip.

10–3). Don't worry about it. When that area is rolled to the center of the frame for quilting, the backing will straighten out. *Note:* The strip should be rolled taut for quilting; but if you are using the running stich, it may be easier to quilt if the strip is loosened slightly.

QUILTING

There are two ways to do the quilting stitch. Most people are familiar with the running stitch. I prefer the less well-known "punch and poke" stitch. I'll discuss both methods in detail, and you can choose the best technique for you. I would urge you to give the "punch and poke" stitch a good try. It takes

longer to perfect, but gives better results on the back of the quilt. where quality shows. A good quilter will usually glance at the surface of a quilt and quickly flip up a corner to see what the stitches look like on the back. There hangs the tale!

The Running Stitch
Most quilters use the running stitch. The right hand holds the needle at an angle and inserts it into the quilt from the top until the tip comes out the back (Fig. 10–4). The left hand stays under the surface of the quilt and "feels" for the needle tip to come through (Fig. 10–5). The tip is then pushed back up to return out the surface of the quilt. You can take from one to three, four or five stitches on the needle. The

Fig. 10–4 Top view of a right-handed quilter doing the running stitch. Notice the "hills" being created by pressure from the hand under the quilt.

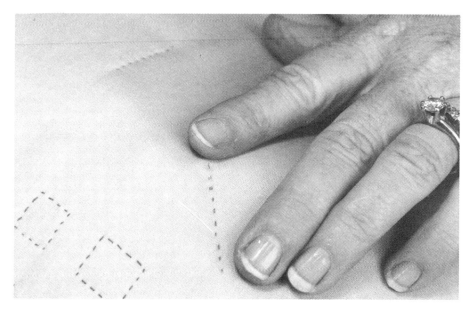

Fig. 10–5 Left index finger feeling the needle point from the underside of the quilt. Some quilters cover this finger with a strip of adhesive tape to prevent pricking.

eye end of the needle is pushed by the middle finger of the right hand until the needle can be grasped and pulled through. This is really the same stitch that was used for piecing, only now the needle is going through three thicknesses. Left-handed quilters would hold the needle in the left hand and have the right hand under the quilt.

"Punch and Poke" Stitch

To do the "punch and poke" stitch, one hand (either one) holds the threaded needle absolutely perpendicular to the fabric, while the index finger "punches" the needle straight down through all three layers (Fig. 10–6). The other hand is underneath the frame; the fingers form a triangle and apply upward pressure on the fabric where the needle will come through (Fig. 10–7). This creates a slight bulge and smooths out the backing. The hand under the frame grasps the needle tip as it emerges out the backing and pulls the needle completely through, but only far enough to turn the needle around and poke it back up to the surface (Fig. 10–8). Usually this means that no more than 2 inches of thread are pulled through to the back. The hand on top then brings the needle out and pulls the thread taut (Fig. 10–9). In essence, each stitch is an individual one.

Fig. 10-6 "Punching" the needle through to the back of the quilt. Notice that the needle is at an absolute right angle to the fabric.

Fig. 10-7 Fingers, forming a triangle, gently push up to receive the needle from the surface.

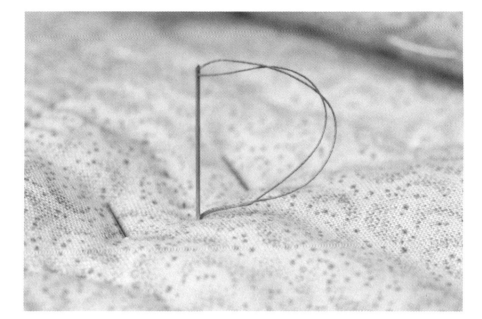

Fig. 10-8 The needle has been pulled through to the back and turned around to go back to the surface. Again, the needle is going into the fabric absolutely straight. Only enough thread is pulled to the back to allow the needle to be turned around.

Fig. 10-9 Receive the needle from the back of the quilt and pull the thread taut. The thumb and forefinger hold the needle, but the thread is pulled by the little finger. This prevents the thread from being frayed where it goes through the eye of the needle.

It is extremely important to remember that one hand always works from the top of the frame and one hand from underneath. The hand on the top *does not* move under the frame to pull the needle through to the back. That would be self-defeating for developing rhythm and speed.

Quilting Thread Tension
You may make very neat quilting stitches, but if the thread tension is not correct, your quilting will not look sharp. If your thread is too tight, the fabric will be puckered. To correct this, do not pull on the thread quite as much when drawing the length through the quilt.

It's not as easy to see if your stitches are too loose. To check the tension, slip the needle under a stitch and pull up. If a loop of thread can be drawn up, the tension is too loose. Pull the thread more taut when quilting.

There should be a happy medium in your thread tension. You want the three layers to be held together firmly, but not so firmly that the quilt puckers. When the quilt is washed, the quilt thread will probably shrink a little and you will notice some puckering.

This is part of the beauty of the quilt, but it should not be confused with quilting stitches that are so tight that they pull the quilt out of shape.

Thimbles

Many women have been taught that they have to use a thimble to be a good seamstress. If you work best with a thimble, terrific! But if you are one of the fifty percent of women who do not use thimbles, don't feel guilty about it. Get on with your quilting, and you will develop a callous on the finger that pushes the needle.

If you do quilt with the running stitch, you don't really have a choice. You must use a thimble or risk destroying the finger that pushes the needle through the quilt. Adhesive tape on the finger that feels for the needle tip will help protect it from constant pricking. Of course, you will not be able to feel the needle tip, but you also won't prick your finger.

The "punch and poke" stitch requires very little finger pressure; therefore, you do not need to use a thimble unless you want to. There is also no need to tape your finger.

In Which Direction Do You Quilt?

If you quilt with the running stitch, there are not many options. A right-handed person quilts from right to left or toward the body. A left-handed person quilts from left to right and can also quilt toward the body.

The "punch and poke" stitch has a tremendous advantage in that it allows you to quilt in any direction, regardless of which hand is used above the frame. At first you will find it easier to quilt in only one direction. If you are right-handed, you will quilt from right to left. When you feel comfortable using the "punch and poke" stitch, you can learn to quilt in any direction, something running-stitch quilters usually can't do.

Starting the Quilting Thread

There are two ways to start the quilting thread. The more traditional method is to use a single thread with a knot. The second method, which I prefer, is to use a double thread and no knot.

Most quilters cut a thread 30 to 36 inches long and put a single knot in one end. The needle is inserted into the backing of the quilt at an angle and pulled out the top at the desired location (Fig. 10–10a). The thread is then pulled so that the knot pops through the back and catches in the batt (Fig. 10–10b).

This method of starting has several disadvantages. When quilting with a thread 30 to 36 inches long, half your time is spent in pulling the thread through the

Fig. 10-10a The needle enters the basted quilt at an angle from the backing.

Fig. 10-10b The knotted thread has been pulled, with a slight jerk, so that the knot passes through the backing fabric and is buried in the batt.

fabric or removing slip knots and tangles. Even worse, the thread begins to fray badly after the first 20 inches have been used, and you end up joining the quilt with thread that may break at any time. You may also have to make several attempts at burying the knot before it catches in the batt, as it tends to pop to the surface very easily. After several washings of the finished quilt, you may also find that some of the knots have popped to the surface, especially if a polyester batt was used.

If you use my method, you'll avoid the problem of knots. Cut a thread 24 inches long and thread the quilting needle so that the thread is doubled. *Note:* You do *not* quilt with a double thread. Poke the needle straight into the top of the quilt where you want the first stitch (Fig. 10–11a). Pull the needle through to the backing while holding on to one 12-inch length of thread. Pull the other 12 inches through to the backing (Fig. 10–11b) and then return the needle to the surface of the quilt. You have taken your first stitch. Lay the loose 12 inches of thread out of the way and continue quilting in the desired direction (Fig. 10–11c). When there are about 2 inches of thread left on the needle, end by weaving it into the batting. Now pick up the 12 inches of loose thread, thread it into the needle and quilt in the opposite direction. You're actually starting in the middle of the 24-inch length of thread and quilting in two different directions.

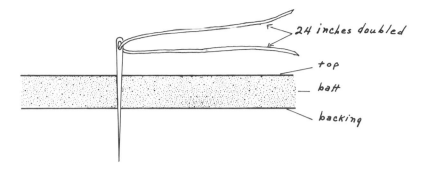

Fig. 10-11a The needle, threaded with a 24-inch length, goes into the basted quilt at the point where you want the first stitch.

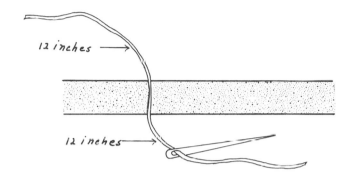

Fig. 10-11b One 12-inch length of thread is pulled through to the back and the other is laid out of the way, to be quilted in after the first half of the thread has been used.

Fig. 10-11c The first half of the thread is quilted into the basted strip in the opposite direction.

What happens if you've quilted a 2-inch square and used only the first half of the thread? Run the threaded needle through the batt to the next quilting line and bring it up at that point (Fig. 10–12). You then continue quilting in the manner just described. Always repeat the first stitch of a shape with your last joining stitch (Fig. 10–13). If this is not done, there will be a skipped stitch on the backing and this will create a bulge.

Ending the Quilting Thread

Always end the thread by weaving it into the batt (Fig. 10–14). Make the last stitch from the top, but instead of going through to the backing, angle the needle into the batt and bring it back up to the surface of the quilt about one inch away (a). Then carefully poke the needle tip into the hole from which the thread emerges and run it into the batt, this time crossing a line of quilting (b). The hole can be enlarged a little if you pull gently on the thread. Repeat this process two

more times, always going in a different direction and crossing a quilted line. Finally, bring the thread out the top of the quilt and cut it off flush with the fabric. The thread end will disappear by dropping back into

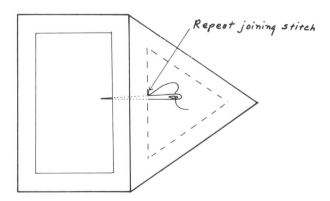

Fig. 10-12 To skip to another patch, run the needle through the batt and bring it up at the desired location.

Fig. 10-13 When ending a quilting line on a shape, repeat the joining stitch or a stitch will be skipped on the backing.

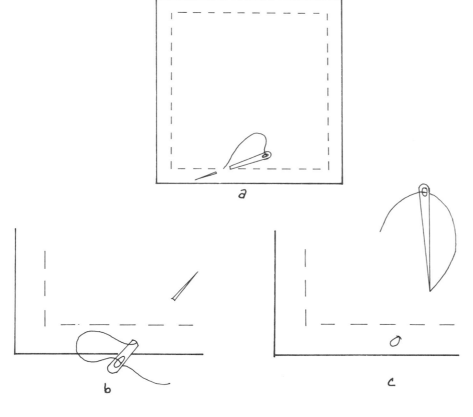

Fig. 10-14 Weaving the thread end. The needle is inserted at an angle and brought up away from the quilting line (a). The needle tip is then put into the hole where the thread emerges (b) and crosses a line of quilting. Repeat step b and pull the thread taut enough so that it drops into the batting (c) each time.

the batt (c). This weaving holds the thread more securely than a knot. _Note:_ Under no circumstances are knots to be visible on the top or backing of the quilt.

Holding the Frame

The quilt-as-you-go frame is very easy to handle. You can sit in any comfortable chair or couch. You're not restricted to a straight-backed chair, as you are with a floor frame.

I usually cross my legs and rest the top dowel on my knee so that both hands are free to quilt. The frame can be turned in any direction you desire. If you are new to quilting or right-handed, you will find it easier to quilt from right to left. When you come to a corner, you can rotate the frame so that you are always quilting from right to left.

If you use the running stitch, I'm sure you can see the advantage of the small frame compared to a large, stationary frame—no more difficult areas to reach.

Quilting at the Strip Edges

The one disadvantage with the quilt-as-you-go method is that you are not able to quilt right up to the seam of the strip while it is still in the frame. If the quilting is brought right up to the seam line, or as close as ¼ inch away it becomes impossible to join the strip seams together (Fig. 10–15). The solution is to quilt to within ½ inch from the strip's edge, pull the needle off the thread and let the thread hang. When the quilted strips are joined together, go back and complete the needed quilting. I generally put the quilt in a 14-inch round quilting hoop for this. It helps to keep the fabric under tension, but it's not really necessary.

Quilting at the Strip Ends

As I've already mentioned, the top, at the 12 inches closest to the dowels, will stretch slightly and the backing will wrinkle (Fig. 10–16). This stretched area must be quilted *into* its area. Remember that the basting rows are only 2 inches apart near the strip ends (see Fig. 9–5). If they were 4 inches apart, it would be more difficult to quilt this excess in. Prior to quilting the stretched area, place straight pins crosswise to the "hills" (Fig. 10–17). The pins will compress the excess until you have quilted that section. When the completed quilt is washed, the fabric will return to its normal shape, if it hasn't already done so due to the quilting.

Fig. 10–15 At the strip's edge, stop quilting ½ inch back from the stitching line and let the quilting threads hang loose. These threads will be quilted in after the strips are joined. This strip is two separate borders. The backing and batting are one piece, but will be cut apart after quilting.

Fig. 10–16 The basted strip removed from the frame to show the stretched top. Notice the rolling "hills and valleys" between the 2-inch basting rows.

Fig. 10-17 Straight pins are placed across the ''hills'' to hold the excess fabric down until that area is quilted.

COMPARING THE QUILTING STITCHES

The running stitch is the fastest way to quilt, the most commonly accepted method and, to a new quilter, *may* be the least frustrating. Nevertheless, I feel that the running stitch has more disadvantages than advantages. Unless you use a very thin batt, the stitches frequently do not go through all layers of the quilt, or they may catch only a few of the backing threads. For really superior quilting, the stitches and spaces should be the same length on both the top and backing.

When using the running stitch, the quilting needle is held as it would be for regular sewing, i.e., parallel to the fabric; therefore, you don't have to retrain your fingers. However, if you have tried the running stitch, you are aware of the amount of lateral pressure needed to push the needle through the quilt. This is almost impossible for someone with arthritis. You should also be aware of the damage the needle hub can do to your finger. If you use the running stitch, you must also use a thimble.

Admittedly, "punch and poke" quilting has some disadvantages, but since these are mostly involved with the learning process, I feel the results far outweigh the inconveniences. Your major task will be to train the hand underneath the frame to return the needle in the spot where you want it. When I was learning, I found that I practiced for five hours before I was able to hit the quilting line from below with any consistency.

I'm sure that with just a little practice you will be extremely happy with the quilting stitches on the top of the quilt, but the quilting stitches on the backing will be another matter. The stitches usually come out unevenly spaced or on the diagonal. To correct this, train your fingers to hold the needle exactly perpendicular to the backing fabric. This seems to be the key, but it does require time and practice. To check yourself, poke the needle into the back as you would ordinarily, but don't pull the needle through to the top. Turn the frame over and look at the needle. Is it coming out straight (Fig. 10–8), or is it leaning to one side? If your stitches are on the diagonal on the backing, I can almost guarantee that the needle will be at an angle. Again, train your fingers to hold the needle so that it goes in straight.

While learning the "punch and poke," it's a good idea to use a printed fabric for the backing and a quilting thread that blends with it. For example, if the top is red, white, and blue, use a red print backing and red quilting thread. The red thread will blend into the backing and not be noticeable. Show your friends the top, and don't point out the diagonal stitches on the back. By the time you are finished with the quilt, you will have mastered the "punch and poke." On your next quilt use a solid color backing with contrasting thread, as I do.

The main thing is to give yourself time. Whether you use the running stitch or the "punch and poke," quilting cannot be done overnight. Relax and enjoy it!

Chapter Eleven

Joining and Binding the Quilt

After two strips have been quilted, as detailed in Chapter 10, they can be joined. This is one of the exciting advantages of quilt-as-you-go. You actually get to see a finished portion of the quilt before it is near completion. The following method is used for joining all strips, whether they are strips of blocks, with or without sashing, or a border to the completed interior of the quilt.

JOINING STRIPS

The Quilt Top
Carefully remove the basting rows if you have not already done so. Trim away any loose threads or uneven seams. Place the two strips to be joined right sides together. Match the long edges. Fold the batt and backing down and out of the way. Pin the quilt top seam on the pencil lines of both strips, just as you did when piecing small patches together (Fig. 11–1). Pin at the beginning corners of the strips and at the intersections of the first block and sash. Pin the interior portions of the block seam line together. Do not

attempt to pin from one strip end to the other. Unless you pin in small sections (each block separately), misalignment may occur. Piece this top seam with a running stitch as you did for all previous piecing. Make sure the stitching is on both pencil lines and that the block intersections of both strips are accurately matched. Do not sew down any seam allowances; sew through them at seam-line level as you did in prior piecing (see Chapter 5: Joining Multiple Edges [Flopping]). When the entire seam line has been sewn, press the seam allowances to one side with your finger. Choose whichever side will allow the cloth to lie flat, and be consistent on the entire quilt.

The Batt
The batt is joined next. It is first trimmed and then whipstitched together. Do not allow the batts from the strips to overlap, or the seam allowance area will be thicker than the rest of the quilt. There are two methods of trimming batts. Use whichever you prefer.

I prefer the first method, which is to trim each batt edge so that they overlap ½ inch. Carefully trim one-half of the batt thickness from the bottom of one batt and one-half of the batt thickness from the top of the

Fig. 11-1 Place two quilted strips with right sides together. Fold the backing and batting out of the way, and pin on both stitching lines.

Fig. 11-2 a: Trim the batt so it overlaps ½ inch. b: Trim one-half of the batt thickness from the top of one batt and one-half the thickness from the bottom of the other batt.

other batt (Fig. 11–2). By trimming and overlapping, the batt is still only one layer thick; yet it seems to "stick" together better. The second method is to butt the edges. Trim both batts so that the edges just touch (Fig. 11–3).

After trimming, the batt edges must be joined together; otherwise, the batt will pull away from the seam line. Whipstitch the batt, using a single, knotted, white, #50 thread (Fig. 11–4). The stitches should be about ½ inch apart and should go only through the batt. This step eliminates the need to outline quilt a seam where the strips are joined.

The Quilt Backing

Trim the raw edges of the backing. Make sure that there are no loose fabric threads on the batt. Lay the

Fig. 11-3 Trim both batts so that the edges just butt together.

seam allowance of one strip down flat. Do not fold it under (Fig. 11–5). Lay the adjoining seam allowance on top and fold the raw edge under for ¼ inch (Fig. 11–6). Pin in place. This seam should be directly over the seam on the quilt top (Fig. 11–7). This can be checked by placing your thumb on the pinned backing seam and your index finger on the sewn top seam. If the backing seam is not directly over the top seam, remove the pins and shift the seam allowance until they do match. Pin the entire seam line in this manner.

Using a single, knotted thread of matching color, sew the backing seam line with the same stitch used for applique (Figs. 7–8 and 7–9). The stitches should be a scant ¼ inch apart. If they are any farther apart, the backing seam line will not lie flat. Take care not to stitch into the quilt top, but do try to catch the batt. This way you can be sure that the joined batt will not shift. The entire strip is now joined.

Border Corners

There are two types of corners—lapped and mitered. The lapped corners need no special handling, since they are all straight pieces. It doesn't matter whether

Fig. 11-4 Whipstitch the trimmed batt together. This eliminates having to outline quilt that seam unless you want to.

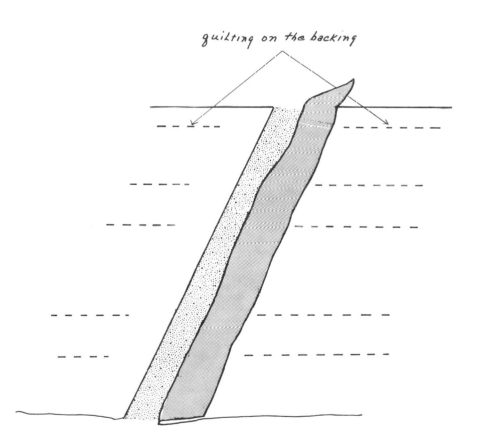

quilting on the backing

Fig. 11-5 Lay one backing strip seam allowance down flat.

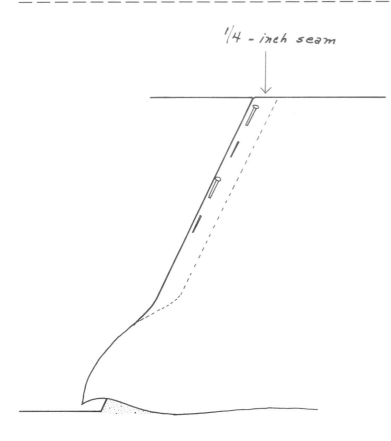

Fig. 11-6 Lay the adjoining seam allowance over it and fold the seam under for ¼ inch. Pin in place.

you join the top and bottom or the sides first (see Fig. 4–27). In either case, it is straight seam joining as I have just discussed.

Joining mitered corners is not really difficult. Pin and then sew the long quilt top seam first; let the corners hang loose. Start and end the batt whip-stitching and the backing stitching about 2 inches in from where the corner miter begins. This lets you get to the mitered top seam allowance. Pin and sew the mitered top together. Press the seam allowance to one side with your finger. Trim and join the batt, being

Fig. 11-7 The backing seam should be directly over the corresponding top seam.

sure you whip the 2-inch unsewn area. Fold the quilt backing as you did for the straight seam. Pin in place. Check to make sure that the backing seam is over the top seam (see Fig. 11–7). Sew the seam, including the 2-inch unsewn area. When handling a miter, be very careful that the fabric is not pulled out of shape. The intersections of the mitered corners and straight seams should all match and lie flat. Study the corners of Color Figs. 1 and 7.

BINDING THE QUILT

Binding—the last stage. Completion is near! There are a few facts that pertain to all quilt binding, whether you are using separate binding or self-binding. First, binding is the portion of the quilt that wears out first. For this reason, I recommend a doubled binding. Second, the binding should be made from the same fabric used in the body of the quilt. Do not use ready-made quilt binding that does not match. Frequently the material is of too light a weave and will not stand up to wear. Purchased binding may save a little time and effort, but after all the work you've already invested, it isn't worth it! Third, not all separate bindings must be cut on the bias, only those for quilts with curved edges. If the quilt edge is straight, the binding can be cut across the 45-inch width of fabric.

Figuring and Cutting Separate Binding

Measure the outer edge of two borders to double-check your original measurements. Multiply this figure by 2 for the outer quilt dimensions. Divide this number by 44 inches (width of material without the selvages). Your answer determines how many 44-inch strips need to be cut. For example, if your sampler quilt is 102 inches square, for a total outside edge of 408 inches, when divided by 44, the result is 9.2. I need 9.2 strips, but will cut 10 strips instead of just a portion of one.

Next, strip width has to be determined. I like a binding of ½ inch. Bindings should be between ½ to ¾ inches wide on both the front and back of the quilt. A narrower binding will look skimpy, and if it's too wide, it will take on the appearance of a narrow border. Let's assume you want a ½-inch binding, doubled, with ¼-inch seams. It will require a strip 2½ inches wide (Fig. 11–8). The binding will use 10 strips, each 2½ inches wide, for a total fabric length of 25 inches of 45-inch wide material.

Using a yardstick, measure across the 45-inch width and even off the fabric. Mark 10 rows, each 2½ inches wide, including the seam allowances. Cut the rows apart on the marked lines. Hand or machine sew all 10 strips together into one long strip, using ¼-inch joining seams. Press the seams open. The strips can be mitered together, but I don't find it necessary. Press the entire strip in half, with the wrong sides together. You are now ready to bind the quilt.

Controlling the Binding

If you find dealing with all that length of binding very awkward, you might try my solution. I seal a business-size envelope and cut off each end. Then I fold the binding like a fan, carefully insert in into the envelope and put a rubber band around it to hold the binding in place. The binding can then be pulled out of the envelope as needed (Fig. 11–9).

Sewing on Separate Binding

As soon as the first border is joined to the quilt interior, the edge can be bound. This helps to keep the raw edges from fraying—another quilt-as-you-go advantage.

Separate bindings can either be attached to the backing and rolled to the top or sewn to the top and rolled to the backing. I prefer rolling to the top, but again, it is your choice.

Start sewing the binding on about 6 inches away from the corner, if it is mitered; if it's lapped, start right at the corner. Only the corners are handled differently. The straight edge technique is the same.

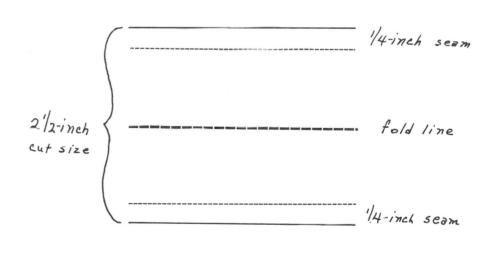

2½-inch cut size

¼-inch seam

fold line

¼-inch seam

Fig. 11–8 A ½-inch finished doubled border requires a 2½-inch wide strip.

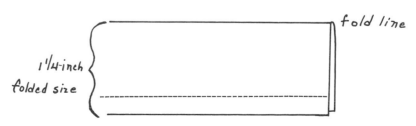

fold line

1¼-inch folded size

Fig. 11-9 The binding is cut, joined, pressed in half, and folded like a fan. It is placed into a sealed envelope that has had both ends cut off. Wrap a rubber band loosely around the bundle.

Fig. 11-10 Set the cut edge of the binding at the edge of the top strip. The batt extends ¼ inch beyond this to provide lift in the finished binding. Pin the binding in place and sew with a running stitch. Make sure that the backing is caught with at least every third or fourth stitch.

Fig. 11-11 Roll the binding to the top and sew with the applique stitch.

There will be a ¼-inch seam allowance of the binding and quilt border. The batt extends ½ inch to provide lift in the bound area (Fig. 11–10).

Pin the binding to the backing (or top) on the ¼-inch seam stitching line. Using a matching, single knotted thread, sew it to the border with a running stitch (see Fig. 11–10). It is not necessary to go through all layers with each stitch, but do so every 3 or 4 stitches. Continue sewing in this manner for the length of the border (see directions below for corners). Roll the folded edge of the binding ¼ inch over the top of the border. Sew it in place, using the applique stitch (Fig. 11–11). Notice that there have been no raw edges to turn under—at last a simple, fast binding application! Refer ahead to Lapped Corners or Mitered Corners before beginning the application.

Self-Binding

Self-binding means bringing the backing fabric over the quilt's top edge to form a binding. When the backing fabric for the border is cut out, this measurement must be included. It is still possible to have a doubled binding. If half the binding is to be on the front, the border must be cut 2 inches wider on that edge and the batt ¼ inch wider to provide the lift needed (Fig. 11–12).

To form the binding, lay the quilt on a table and fold the binding over (wrong sides together) so that there is a ¼-inch seam allowance between the backing and batt (Fig. 11–13). Now bring the folded edge over to the ¼-inch stitching line (Fig. 11–14). Pin in place and sew down with your applique stitch. Do not stitch all the way through the layers, but just into the batt. No stitches should show on the backing.

BINDING CORNERS

The binding corners should be turned in the same direction as the border corners. If the border corners were lapped, the binding must be lapped and in the same direction. If border corners are mitered, miter the binding corners (Fig. 11–15).

Lapped Corners (Separate Binding)

Lapped binding is applied as detailed above, but the application starts right at the corner. The first binding is applied completely from corner to corner. The joining binding is started so that ½ inch of binding extends beyond the corner and is sewn only to the backing with a running stitch. Cut away the excess fabric (Fig. 11–16). Fold in the ½-inch extension over the raw edge (Fig. 11–17). Fold the binding over the

Fig. 11-12 Determining the additional measurement needed for self-binding when using the backing fabric.

Fig. 11-13 Double the self-binding so that ¼ inch lies between the backing and batt.

Fig. 11-14 Roll the folded edge over the quilt's raw edge. Pin in place and sew down with the applique stitch.

top of the quilt, pin and sew (Fig. 11–18). Make sure this corner fold is closed with close, invisible stitches. Repeat for each corner.

Lapped Corners (Self-binding)

The end product is basically the same for self-binding. Fold and stitch the first binding. Next, fold the adjoining binding over the required depth and cut away a ¼-inch rectangle, as detailed in Fig. 11–16. Close the end with small, invisible whipstitches as you continue to sew the binding. Repeat for each corner.

Mitered Corners (Separate Binding)

Mitered corners are never started or ended at a corner (see Sewing on Separate Binding). They are sewn on with one long strip of fabric. Attach the first side of

mitered

lapped

right

wrong

Fig. 11-15 Turn the binding corners in the same direction as the border.

remove excess

Fig. 11-16 Cut away the excess bulk for a lapped binding.

Fig. 11-17 Fold in the first edge of the lapped corner. Pin.

the strip with a running stitch. Do not roll the strip over to the quilt front until the corner has been turned. Sew the binding with a running stitch to where the ¼-inch pencil lines meet on the wrong side of the fabric. Backstitch and knot the thread (Fig. 11–19). Do not cut the binding or thread. Fold the binding directly back on itself so that the fold is on the cut edge of the top (Fig. 11–20). Now lay the binding along the next edge to be bound, on its cut edge (Fig. 11–21). A mitered fold and pleat have been formed. Hold the binding in place and pull the pleat to the

surface (Fig. 11–22). Stitch through the pleat at seam-line level and backstitch on that side of the pleat (Fig. 11–23). Continue sewing the binding on with a running stitch. When you have sewn 3 to 4 inches past the corner, go back and roll the binding to the front of the quilt and stitch it down. When the corner is folded over, a miter will automatically form on the backing of the binding (Fig. 11–24). Fold the top of the binding in on one edge and pin (Fig. 11–25). Fold the second edge in so that an exact miter is formed (Fig. 11–26). Whipstitch both top and back binding miters

Fig. 11-18 Make the final fold. Pin and stitch very closely.

Fig. 11-19 Sew the first edge of the mitered binding up to the penciled corner (marked on the wrong side of the fabric). Backstitch and knot the thread but *do not* cut it. (The pencil line is shown on the right side of the example for clarity.)

Fig. 11-20 Fold the binding back on itself. The fold is on the cut edge of the top.

Fig. 11-21 Now lay the binding along the next edge to be bound so that the binding's stitching line is over the penciled line of the border.

Fig. 11-22 Hold the binding in place and pull the pleat to the surface. The pin marks the stitching line on the top border.

Fig. 11-23 Stitch through the pleat and backstitch. Continue sewing the binding down the edge.

Fig. 11-24 When the binding is rolled to the front, a mitered corner will automatically form on the backing.

Fig. 11-25 Fold the first edge of the binding corner and pin it in place.

Fig. 11-26 Fold the corner over so that the point is on the binding seam-line intersection. Pin in place.

Fig. 11-27 Fold over the binding corners so that an exact, matching miter forms. Pin in place. Sew with invisible stitches.

Fig. 11-28 A completed binding miter.

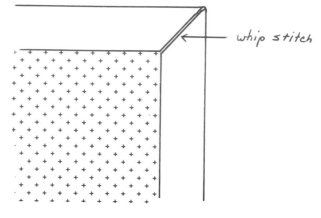

Fig. 11-29 Fold the corner of self-binding over to the penciled corner so that a triangle forms.

Fig. 11-30 Fold each edge in to form a perfect miter. Pin in place and sew with applique stitches so that no raw edges or stitches show.

in place as the binding is being sewn down (Fig. 11–27). Repeat for each corner. You've completed a perfect miter in one operation (Fig. 11–28).

Mitered Corners (Self-Binding)
Fold one corner of the binding ¼ inch under the batt and cut away a rectangle of fabric as detailed in Fig. 11–16. Fold under the other binding edge. Fold the corner point down to the ¼-inch binding seam-line intersection so that a triangle forms (Fig. 11–29). Pin in place. Fold over each edge of the binding so that an exact miter forms (Fig. 11–30). Pin in place and sew with invisible stitches as the binding is stitched down. Repeat for each corner.

Chapter Twelve

Drafting Layouts and Figuring Yardage

In the preceding eleven chapters, I have dealt with the quilting basics. Each separate technique, whether it is simple piecing, involved piecing, applique, strip assembly, or quilting, applies to all quilts including the samplers, which you might want to make for a first project. Traditionally made in needlepoint, crewel, embroidery, and quilting the sampler is a learning tool that can be referred to for handling a particular problem. Even more important, it can be used as a sample of how *not* to do something. For the seasoned quilter, a sampler showing depth of ability can also be a record of high accomplishment. It is, however, only one of thousands of quilt possiblities. You may choose, instead, to try a wall hanging or a king-size quilt. The techniques learned in this book will be exactly the same for any project.

This chapter will deal with planning and drafting, whether it is for a quilt or a pillow. When my love affair with quilts began, I discovered that I had to contend with math—my worst subject in school—or

face the fact that I would always be sadly short of fabric. I hope you are not a "numbers ninny" as I am, but if you are, I have tried to make the information as simple as possible.

QUILT LAYOUTS

Once you have measured the bed and determined how large your quilt is to be (see Chapter 4), you will need to make a quilt layout. This is a finished drawing of the quilt. It can be a rough sketch or a very detailed drawing with fabric glued to the design. Whichever you choose to make, be sure to keep it where it can be found! It is no good if misplaced. I keep mine in a binder with all details noted, including quilt size, fabric samples, amount of fabric purchased, cost of the fabric and the number of patches that have been cut. The last is listed because I may not work on that quilt

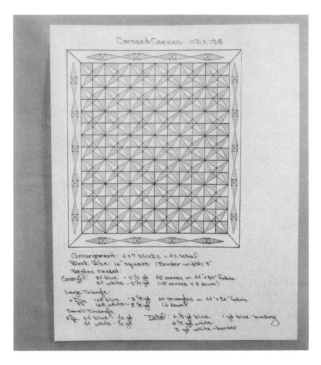

Fig. 12-1 The layout and yardage notes that I made for my Crossed Canoes quilt.

for some time and I tend to forget how much cutting remains to be done (Fig. 12–1).

Block Arrangement and Size

How do you determine the best way to arrange blocks? It is really a matter of personal preference; no one way is necessarily right. Fig. 12–2 shows a quilt with a 16-inch block size and block-to-block assembly. Notice how the sashed quilt (Fig. 12–3) has a pattern that has been exploded in size, which results in a large, circular, secondary pattern. The block-to-block assembly has a fairly small circle with a star in the center as its secondary pattern.

After you've chosen your block arrangement, you'll need to determine the size of the block. Remember—the smaller the block the smaller the patches and the more blocks needed. I generally use a 14- to 16-inch block, because I don't like to handle tiny patches. If your quilt is to fit a certain bed, this will take some figuring. Answering the following questions will help you plan your quilt.

1. Will the quilt be used with a skirt or will it fall to the floor?

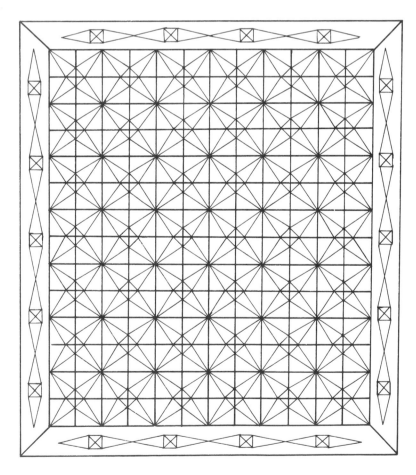

Fig. 12-2 Crossed Canoes layout. Photocopy the layout several times and experiment with colored pencils to determine color placement.

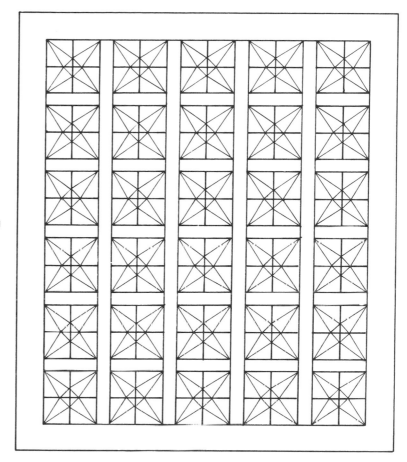

Fig. 12-3 Crossed Canoes with sashing layout.

2. What is the block arrangement: sashing, block-to-block, or alternate block?

3. Do you want the quilt to tuck under the pillows?

4. Do you want a single, double, or triple border? Or maybe no border at all?

5. Will the border be pieced, appliqued, or plain? This doesn't affect the size, but will change the amount of fabric needed.

Once these questions are answered, block size can be determined. Block-to-block assembly is the easiest to plan, so we will work with my Crossed Canoes in Fig. 12–2. I wanted a king to the floor with a single border and block-to-block assembly. I needed a total quilt size of 112 by 128 inches. Divide both these numbers by a variety of possible block sizes (12, 13, 14, 15, 16) to see which number best goes into both the width and length measurements. It turns out to be 16. It divides into 112 seven times and into 128 eight times. Since I want a single border, I can divide the 16-inch block size into two and have an 8-inch bor-

der. This means there will be one less block in both width and length. My quilt layout will be a 6 by 7 block arrangement with 8-inch borders and 16-inch block. See Fig. 12–2.

Figuring a quilt layout becomes more complicated with sashing. If I had wanted to use sash, it would have been 4 inches wide and the quilt would have had one less block in both width and length. The quilt would also have been 4 inches longer. Can you tell why? Four sashes, each 4 inches wide, total 16 inches or one block. One block would be removed from the above quilt width, but five sashes would be used between six blocks for a total length increase of 20 inches. The overall length would be increased to 132 inches. This extra 4 inches could be used as pillow tuck (Fig. 12–3).

Inaccurate Blocks

Before dealing with drafting, I want to again stress the importance of pattern accuracy (see Chapter 3: Checking Pattern Accuracy). I have seen any number of students who have been totally defeated by geometric piecing because nothing ever fits. Usually, the culprit is not the stitcher but the pattern. Don't trust any pattern! Remember, a mistake of only ⅛ inch can cause complete disaster. Do take the time to measure your pattern, using the directions given at the beginning of Chapter 3.

What if a friend wants a pattern of yours? Photocopying can distort a pattern. Don't use a machine with a curved glass plate; it magnifies on the outer edges and not in the center. Be sure you always check your copy against the original. And please remember that photocopying out of books for resale or general distribution is illegal.

Drafting Supplies

No expensive equipment is needed for good drafting, but a few basics are essential. These are available at any art supply or stationery store. Before you buy, check all the measuring supplies against one another. You may find that one company's inch may not be another company's inch.

Graph paper: 1-inch squares divided into a grid pattern. Grids are available in 4, 6, 8, and 10. The last is the easiest to work with.

Gridded ruler: this ruler is divided into ⅛-inch segments and is 2 inches wide and 18 inches long.

Sharp, fine, lead pencil.

Black felt-tip pen with a fine point.

Block Drafting

Make all drawings on graph paper, using a ruler as a straight-edge guide. It is usually not necessary to draft an entire block, but only a portion of it. Circles generally require full block drafting. Study the block to be drafted to see if it is a four, five, seven, or nine patch.

We will work with the Crossed Canoes block and assume that you have seen a completed quilt but do not have a pattern. This a four patch and only a quarter of the block needs to be drafted. The block is to be 16 inches square (see Block Arrangement and Size). Make an 8-inch-square on the graph paper by carefully following the grid lines with a ruler. Study the complete block in Figure 12–4. The first line to be drawn will be the base of the long triangle (Canoe). Question: How long should that line be? Answer: Find out by trial and error and decide by what looks good to you. Make a dot 4 inches out from a corner on each of two converging lines and connect them with a straight line (Fig. 12–5a). Next draw a straight line from each of these dots to the opposite corner (Fig. 12–5b). A long triangle has been formed. How does it look (Fig. 12–6)? Not very balanced. Who wants a fat canoe that looks as if it might sink! Try again with a 1½-inch base (Fig. 12–7). This canoe is

Fig. 12-4 Crossed Canoes. It is generally a two-color block, but more colors can be used if so desired.

so thin that no one could fit in it! You will find that a 2½-inch base seams to be the best measurement, and the canoe looks in proportion.

It's much easier if you do have a pattern which gives the general proportions. You'll only need to

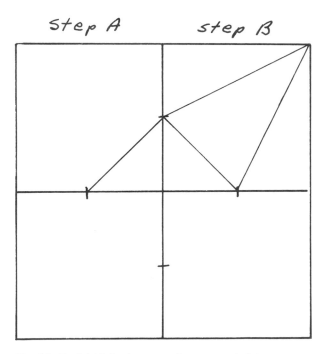

Fig. 12-5 (a) Make base marks an equal distance from the block center. Connect with a straight line. (b) Connect the base marks to the block's outer corner with straight lines.

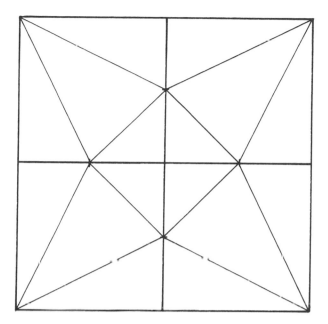

Fig. 12-6 This Crossed Canoes has a 4-inch base and looks too thick and heavy to float.

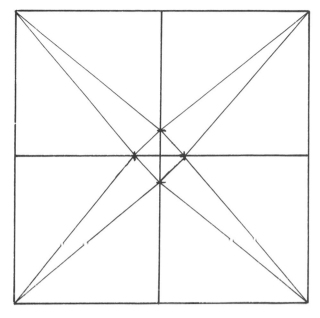

Fig. 12-7 A Crossed Canoes with a 2-inch base looks as if it were meant for pencil-people!

"even them up." Use the original templates and lay each piece on the graph paper in the location in which it will be pieced. This is a pattern for Our Village Green (Fig. 12–8). Do some patches overlap or have gaps between them? Make all necessary corrections, using a ruler and pencil on graph paper, and proceed as directed below.

When your pattern has been carefully drafted, it can be transferred to template material. If Mylar acetate is used, lay it over the drafted pattern and using a ruler as guide, trace the pattern onto the Mylar. Cut out. If the template material is not transparent, make a paper duplicate of the drafted design and cut it apart. Lay each piece on the template material and trace around it. Cut out (see Chapter 3: Making Templates).

Mark each template with the block name and size. I keep my templates together with paper clips and put each block in a separate, labeled envelope. Keep the graphed original just in case you lose the template.

Fig. 12-8 Checking a pattern of uncertain accuracy. Make paper templates and lay them in a block drawn to the required size. If everything fits, the pattern is accurate. If not, redraft.

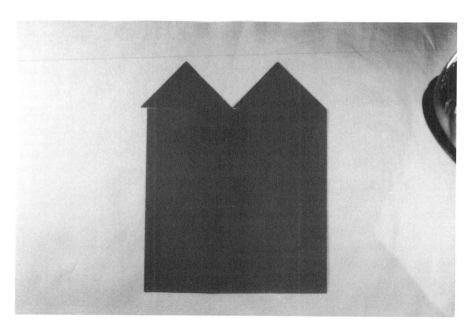

FIGURING YARDAGE

Crossed Canoes is a simple four-patch, two-color design. When it's used in a block-to-block assembly (Fig. 12–2) it's easy to figure yardage amounts. All yardage amounts are determined in the following manner, whether you are figuring yardage for a single block or a large sampler quilt.

Questions to answer (Crossed Canoes layout used as an example [Fig. 12–2]):

1. How many blocks in the quilt? Six by seven assembly, 42-block total.

2. How many colors in each block? Two. Blue and white.

3. Is the block evenly divided? Yes. The same amounts of blue and white are used.

4. How many different shapes are in the block? Three. A long triangle (canoe), a small right-angle triangle, a large right-angle triangle.

5. How many of each color and shape need to be cut for each block? Blue: 2 long triangles (canoe), 2 small triangles, and 4 large triangles (2 cut reversed). White: the same amounts as the blue.

6. How many of each patch are needed for the total quilt? Multiply 42 (number of blocks in the quilt) times each of the answers in Question 5: 42×2 long triangles = 84; 42×2 small triangles = 84; 42×4 large triangles = 168. These amounts will be needed in both blue and white.

Now that the total number of patches is known, yardage must be figured. We will work with 45-inch wide material with the selvages cut off, for a total working width of 44 inches.

First, you must determine how the templates will be placed on the material (see Chapter 3: Positioning Templates). Then measure the longest and widest points of all templates. In all previous discussions of measurements, I have talked in finished sizes, usually ignoring seam allowances. These ¼-inch seams must now be added to each patch for a total addition of ½ inch; otherwise, you will be grossly short of fabric.

Questions to answer (continued):

7. How many templates of a single shape can be cut out of a single row across the 44-inch material? To get the answer, divide the width of the template (seams included) into 44 inches. Long triangle (4-inch wide): $44 \div 4 = 11$. You can get 11 canoes across. You need a total of 84 canoes. Divide the total number of canoes needed by the number of canoes per row: $84 \div 11 = 7.6$ or 8 rows. The triangle is 10

inches long. The number of rows must be multiplied by the length of the patch: $8 \times 10 = 80$ inches. Since the fabric is purchased by the yard and not the inch, it must be converted: $80 \div 36 = 2.2$ yards. I would buy 2.5 yards of both blue and white for the canoes.

Figure the yardage needed for the two remaining patches to see if you get the answers I have.

Large triangle

Total needed: 168
Size: 6 by 8½ inches
Number in a row: $44 \div 6 = 7.3$ or 7 patches in a row
Number of rows needed: $168 \div 7 = 24$ rows needed
Number of rows times patch length: $24 \times 8½ = 204$ inches
Convert to yards: $204 \div 36 = 5.7$ yards. Buy 5⅞ yards

Small triangle

Total needed: 84
Size: 3 by 3
Number in a row: $44 \div 3 = 14.7$ or 14 patches in a row
Number of rows needed: $84 \div 14 = 6$ rows needed
Number of rows times patch length: $6 \times 3 = 18$ inches
Convert to yards: $18 \div 36 = .5$ or ½ yard

Border Yardage

Border yardage is figured in the same manner, except that you work with larger units. First, you must determine in what direction to cut the borders. If the longest border measurement is cut the length of the fabric, it will not need to be pieced. If cut selvage to selvage, there will be seams every 44 inches. See Chapter 4: Cutting Methods, for a detailed explanation and diagrams. My choice is determined by width of border, the amount of leftover fabric that can be used for piecing, and the amount of money I have at the time.

The borders are 8½ inches (cut size) and the quilt is 112 by 128 inches. I can cut the four borders down the length of the material (cutting method 1) without having to piece. The combined cut border width totals 34 inches and leaves a 10-inch strip for piecing (Fig. 12–9). Calculate with the longest border: $128.5 \div 36 = 3.6$ yards for border fabric.

After all of the above very detailed figuring, including the canoes I will applique in the border, it is important to realize that the final figures are only estimates. They do not take into account: mistakes, alterations in color placement, or fabric shrinkage during washing. In the final analysis, I know how much I need down to the last inch. And then I buy more! For Crossed Canoes, I bought a yard more of both blue and white. It is better to have too much fabric than to discover too late that you've made a mistake.

Do cut borders and background blocks, if any, to begin with. Next, piece one block to see how much fabric is actually used. Do you have enough to finish the remaining blocks? This double-checks the yardage estimates and shows me that I didn't make any math errors.

Fig. 12-9
Cutting method 1 for a Crossed Canoes border that is 8 inches wide.

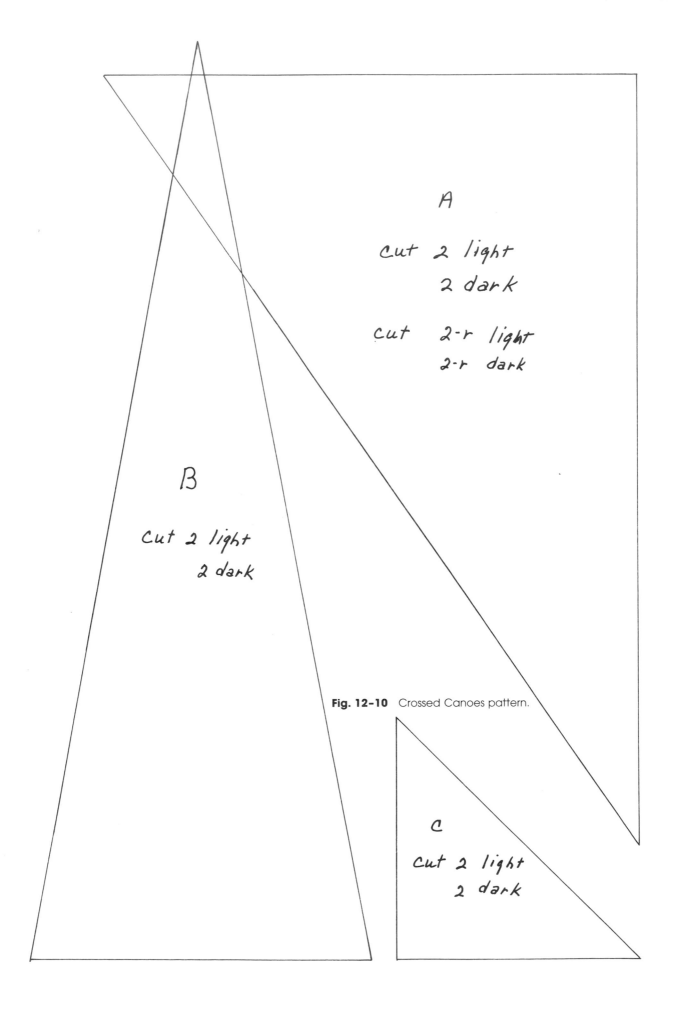

A

Cut 2 light
2 dark

Cut 2-r light
2-r dark

B

Cut 2 light
2 dark

Fig. 12-10 Crossed Canoes pattern.

C
Cut 2 light
2 dark

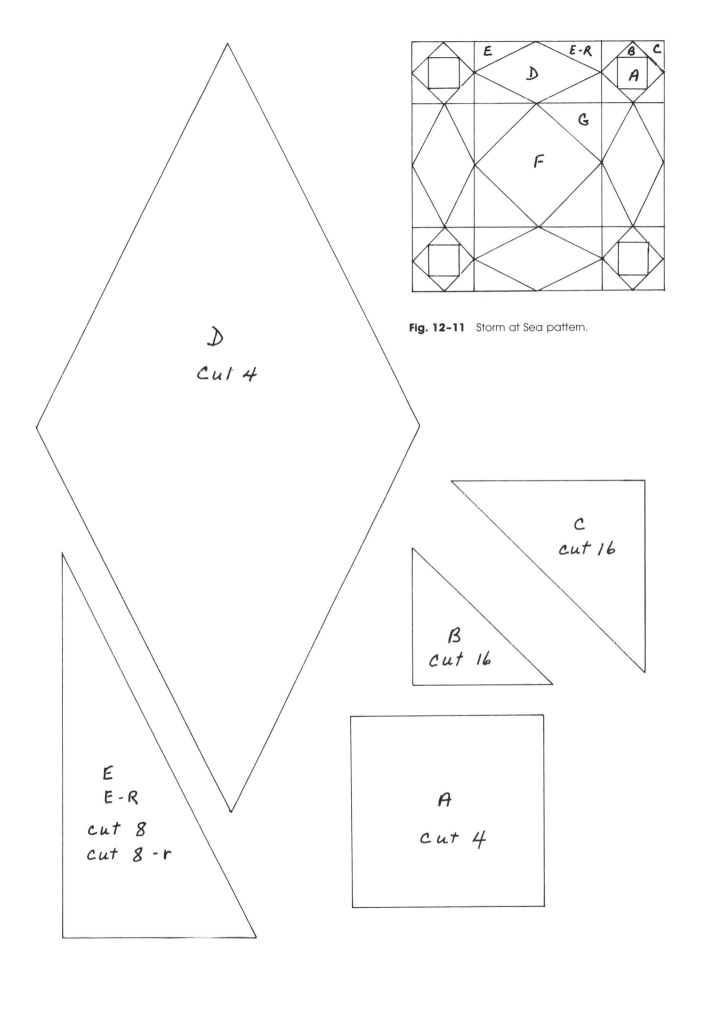

Fig. 12-11 Storm at Sea pattern.

D

Cut 4

C

cut 16

B

Cut 16

E

E-R

cut 8

cut 8-r

A

cut 4

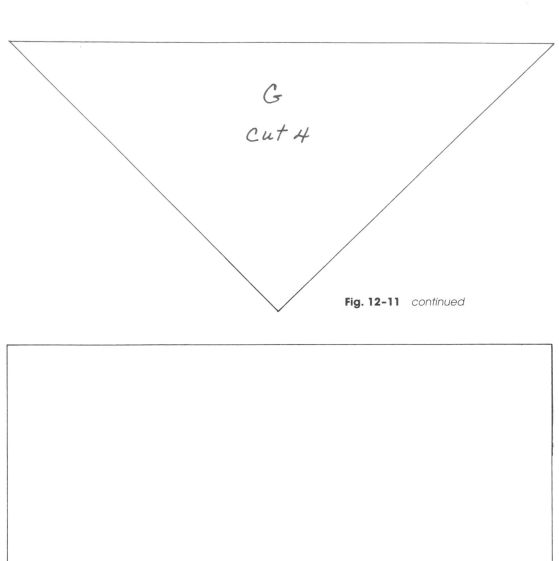

G

Cut 4

Fig. 12-11 *continued*

F

Cut 1

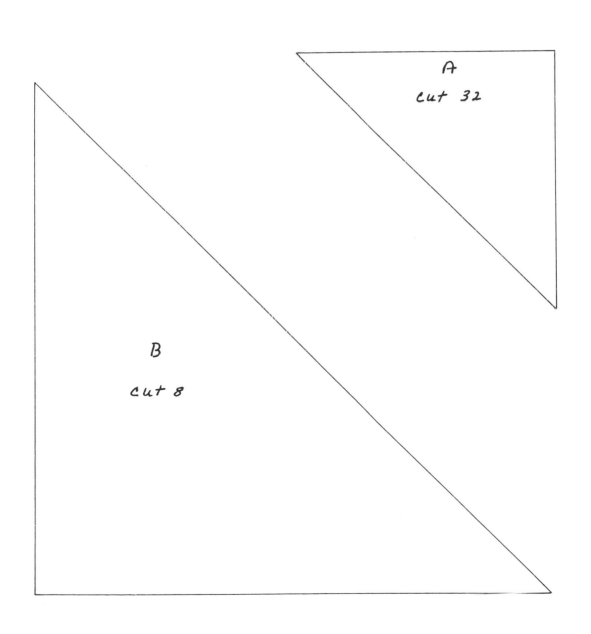

Fig. 12-12 Corn and Beans pattern.

A
cut 32

B
cut 8

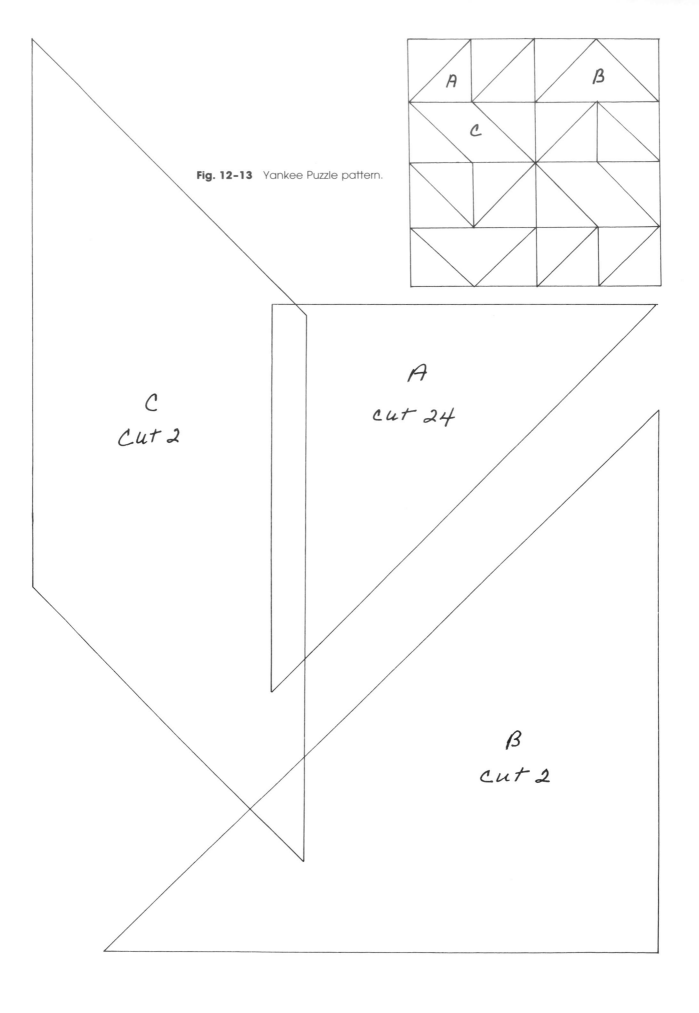

Fig. 12-13 Yankee Puzzle pattern.

A
cut 24

C
Cut 2

B
cut 2

Chapter Thirteen

Wall Quilts with a Single Design Motif

Quilts moved from beds to walls after the American Bicentennial in 1976. As quiltmaking became more popular, quilters soon realized that making full-sized quilts greatly limited their creative output. By the early 1980s, warmth was not necessarily the primary reason for their construction. Quilters made more quilts of smaller sizes, and artistic accomplishment became a quilt's reason for existence. Fabric color, its varying textures, and a needle and thread replaced the painter's brush and canvas in the hands of the quilt artist.

Now that you have learned the basic techniques of quiltmaking, it is time to explore designing a wall quilt: to become a quilt artist. Quilts made from a single patch pattern can be developed into elaborate designs by varying color. The colored edge of a fabric patch can be softened, changed, or made to disappear by the color and pattern design of the neighboring patches. Choosing fabrics in the same way a painter selects paints explodes the design possibilities for a quilter.

There are two wall quilts in this chapter. Both deal with the use of color and how your choices determine the final design of the quilt. While there are certainly many ways to approach designing a quilt, no one way is best, only what works for that particular project and the artist.

The first wall quilt is a pieced, single pattern repeat, with design and form developing from the use of fabric color/pattern changes. The second incorporates a three-inch square patch, using the color experience gained in working with the first wall quilt, but now adding an applique design overlay and experimenting with color changes when fabric is layered.

DESIGNING A WALL QUILT

There is more to making a quilt than choosing fabrics. The newsman's basic six questions, plus one of my own—cost—apply to quiltmaking and need to be answered.

1. Who? The intended recipient is . . . ?

2. What? Is it to be a wall quilt, bed quilt or ?

3. Where? Where is it going to hang?

4. When? Is there a deadline?

5. Why? Do you want to learn a new technique, make a gift, or decorate a spot in your home?

6. How? Is it to be assembled quilt-as-you-go or full size? Will the shape present hanging problems?

7. Cost? Buying seven new fabrics is much different than needing twenty-seven new fabrics.

Designing: Starting from Scratch

The following is a detailed account of the thought process and designing of the Raindrops wall quilt for this book (See color section Figures 11 and 12).

1. Who? For the *Quilt-As-You-Go* reader who has technical experience and wants to begin designing.

2. What? A wall quilt with approximately 36- to 42-inch outer measurements. Use of a single patch repeat.

3. Where? Intended for general display, similar to a painting.

4. When? As soon as possible.

5. Why? To give experience to a student on how to handle a larger number of fabric colors, and the confidence to try designing an original project.

6. How? It must have some straight line(s) for attaching into the quilt-as-you-go frame.

7. Cost? The small size will contain the costs, but the final price will be determined by the number of different fabrics used in the quilt. (Try to use as many fabrics already on hand as possible.)

Supplies Needed

1. Graph paper, 10 grids to the inch. This paper comes in various sizes: tablets of 8½ × 11 inch, or 11 × 17, and individual sheets of 24 × 36. It is also available in 4, 8, and 12 grids to the inch. Ten is the most versatile.

2. Lead pencil: .50 mm diameter lead.

3. Kneaded eraser: erases without leaving a residue. This eraser kneads like clay and can be used over and over.

4. Gridded rulers: 2 × 18 inches and 1 × 6 inches.

5. Acetate or stiff paper to make permanent patterns.

6. Scissors, but not the good ones used for fabric.

7. Photocopy machine or tracing paper to duplicate the final design.

8. Glue stick or Scotch tape. Glue stick is better.

9. Colored pencils, watercolor pens, or crayons (crayons smear).

10. A Styrofoam insulation board: 2 by 4 or 8 foot rectangle, 1 or 2 inches thick. These are very inexpensive and are used to pin fabric on. Look in building supply stores.

BEGINNING THE DESIGN PROCESS

Working with the graph paper, lead pencil, and rulers, I started doodling, trying for a shape that would interlock with itself, yet be different enough from other shapes I'd seen. Because of the restricted quilt size, the patch could not be too large or there wouldn't be enough patches in the design to develop any repeat pattern. Too small and it would take forever to make and visually be too busy. I decided against curved edges. See Figure 13–1 for my doodle. It is the original size beside the full-sized patch. I like to work small to get a better perspective, then enlarge.

I liked the interlocked lines, which brought to mind Greek toga trim. This design has a number of advantages when placing color: the color can be in vertical columns, on the diagonal, waved on the diagonal or interwoven. In short, there are a lot of color design possibilities.

Next, enlarge the doodle to full size, but keep the proportions the same scale. My doodle was 3 grids high on the longest leg and 2 grids wide. Working on 10 grids to the inch graph paper, I first enlarged the shape to 3 inches on the long leg (4¼ inches for the total shape) and 1½ inches wide, not 2 inches as the doodle indicates, since I liked those proportions better.

Figuring Quilt Size

How many patches would I need for the quilt's height? Each interlocking shape (two units) is 6 inches high. I want the quilt to be about 40 inches in length. $40 \div 6 = 6.7$ shapes, How many for the width? Each interlocked shape is 1½ inches wide. I want the quilt to be about 25 inches wide. $25 \div 1.5 = 16.7$, then increased to 20 to be larger.

How many total patches needed are determined by multiplying the number of patches in the length by the

Fig. 13-1 Raindrops pattern. The small design to the side is my original-sized doodle for this pattern.

10 grids per inch graph

8.5"

2"

number of patches in the width. Because I don't want to figure with a percentage of a patch, I increased the number of units in the length to 7. 7 × 20 = 140 patches needed for a completed quilt size of 42 × 20 inches.

That's too many for the time I have, and unnecessary to achieve a good design. I repeated the figures for a larger unit and finally decided on an interlocked patch 8.5 inches long and 2 inches wide (notice, I'm back to the original doodle width). This size requires 10 interlocked units in length and 10 interlocked units in width for a total quilt size (minus any border) of 42.5 × 20 inches with 100 patches total. Final

numbers I could live with. In actuality, there are 95 whole patches and 25 partial patches at the top and bottom.

Making the Quilt Layout

Now that the size and proportions of the quilt are finalized, it is time to make a drawing of the quilt layout. Duplicate a portion of the quilt (I draw ¼ of the quilt) on the graph paper; however, the full quilt diagram is provided in Fig. 13–2. If you are working with only a quarter diagram, photocopy it four times and retain the original drawing. Cut the photocopies apart and glue them onto another piece of graph

Fig. 13-2 Raindrops quilt layout. Photocopy this design for color experimentation.

2. Use a single fabric you like and find complementary fabrics to match or contrast with it.

3. Match a preexisting color; i.e., pick fabrics to go with a room's color scheme.

4. Try something different to stretch your creativity.

Once a group of colors is selected, the next task is to figure out where in the design they should go. Use colored pencils or watercolor pens and begin to experiment, coloring the whole quilt photocopies with various color schemes. See the color section Fig. 11 for the Raindrop quilt color experiment.

Hint: For someone new to this type of color experimentation, it might be easier to first work with a single block from the sampler quilt (see color section, Figure 10). What happens to the same patches when they are made dark in one sample and light in another? What recedes and what comes forward? By trying a variety of color possibilities, you can make one area more important than another, spotlight a secondary pattern (see below), and determine what area of the block is to be the most important. It also saves time and wasted fabric.

Remember: Dark colors come forward and are more important, light colors recede and are less important.

SECONDARY PATTERNS

Secondary patterns are patterns that are not obvious in a single-block or sashed quilt, but show up with a block-to-block assembly. One block that I designed to specifically have strong secondary patterns is Twisted Bands (see Fig. 8–21). See also completed sampler quilt (see color section Figs. 1 and 2). I wanted a design element to carry through the entire quilt, and so deliberately placed strong colors in patches A, B and E, and in S and M to develop those secondary patterns.

If the Twisted Bands block only was used in a block to block assembly with the colors chosen in the sample, there would be strong color bands running both vertically and diagonally and the individual block would be hard to detect. Have you ever seen a quilt with such a strong secondary pattern that it was hard to determine the individual block pattern? Locate it by looking at a corner and working out until you find the repeat.

Look at the yellow and lavender floral wall hanging in color section Fig. 6. This is also Twisted Bands. Four blocks were joined block to block, but the quilt-

paper then into the completed design (see Fig. 13–2). Since this double patch is a mirror image, it can be rotated upside down. A design that is not a mirror image or an asymmetrical design would require having a reverse drawing made before photocopying to get a right and left side. Photocopy this new original five to ten times. The designing is complete, you are now ready to work with colors.

Choosing Colors

Picking a color scheme for this wall quilt was as easy as hearing my daughter say, "Mom, the design looks like raindrops." The design suddenly had a blue color *and* a name, Raindrops. If a daughter isn't handy, there are other ways to choose a color scheme. Reread Chapter 2 for color basics information.

1. The design itself suggests colors.

maker chose to rotate each block one-quarter turn and use colors that did not enhance the color bands as I envisioned them when designing the block. To see another quilter's version of what a finished block or quilt should look like is an exciting aspect of quilting.

Picking the Fabrics

Coloring the quilt diagram is easier than choosing the fabrics to represent the colors. Keep in mind that what you have colored in *may not* work in fabric. Fabric patterns, change in color, and patch size, can affect the overall look. I found that too many different colors, though accurately reflecting my example, confused the eye. I eliminated some colors and moved others together to give a stronger sense of diagonal movement.

ASSEMBLING RAINDROPS

Once fabric placement is decided upon (see color section Fig. 11), begin piecing. The interlocking patches can be flopped and sewn with one thread. First, *clip* into each diagonal corner, to within ⅛ inch of the pencil line. Sew toward the turn and backstitch at the corner, flop, stitch through the seam and backstitch at the beginning of the long center seam (this is the tricky part), and then repeat the flopping process at the bottom diagonal turn. Join the next patch on the long diagonal, being careful not to stretch the fabric out of shape.

Finish piecing each interlocking row. Press each row, with the diagonal seams facing in alternate directions (row 1 up, row 2 down, row 3 up, etc). This helps to accurately join the intersecting row seams. Use extreme caution when pressing each interlocking row. The patches can be permanently stretched out of shape. Also, press from the right side to eliminate any seam fold-overs.

Join the pieced rows together into the completed top (match those intersecting seams) and press the vertical seams. Border, quilt, and bind the wall hanging as described in earlier chapters. I chose to use random quilting lines to emphasize the diagonal raindrops, ignoring the interlocked patch shape. Your choices could be entirely different.

COLOR AS A DESIGN ELEMENT: THE DESIGN PROCESS FOR FOREST SPHERES

In Forest Spheres there are only two shapes, a circle and a square. The piecing and applique are quite straightforward; the technical assembly should not present any problems. The challenges are in choosing and placing color.

I wanted a simple pattern that would not fight with an applique design placed on top. One that would be simple and fast to piece and would allow easy movement of fabric patches (that meant no tiny triangles) when arranging colors. I chose a 3-inch square, and assembled 6 blocks by 13 blocks for a finished size of 18 inches by 39 inches.

The Designing Steps

1. Graph the basic 6 by 13 block shape on graph paper. I used 10 to the inch grid paper with 3 grids equaling one square. See Figure 13–3 for the basic shape.

2. I wanted the design to be horizontal and the light source to come from high on the left.

3. Colors? Yellows changing to deep greens with a bit of red for spice. See the color section, Fig. 14, for my color sample. The first try worked, since I had a specific picture in my mind of the finished product.

4. Now for the applique design. Something floral. I doodled on a photocopied grid design a number of times until I had three floral shapes that I liked. See Fig. 13–4.

Remember: Odd numbers (3, 5, 7) look more balanced than even numbers.

5. The floral shapes were cut out and lined up on the colored grid pattern, glued in place, then colored so that the applique design would stand out from the background (see Color Section Figure 14).

6. The square and floral applique templates were made next. See Figs. 13–3 and Fig. 13–7. See also Chapter 3: Patterns and Templates, for review if needed.

7. Needed are 78 squares of fabrics in your color choice, ranging from lights to darkest darks (see below for color selection). Choose enough contrasting or complementary colors to give interest. It is easiest to start with some colors you like and cut more as you arrange the pieced background. *Do not sew anything together.* Also, review Chapter 2 before beginning.

8. Stand the Styrofoam board on a table at eye level and pin each square to the board with one pin stabbed straight into the foam. Start placing the lightest patches first and work down and out, gradually using darker patches until the darkest part of the background is completed. Step back frequently to see if the colors are blending to your satisfaction. Does any patch jump out? Do you like that look or should

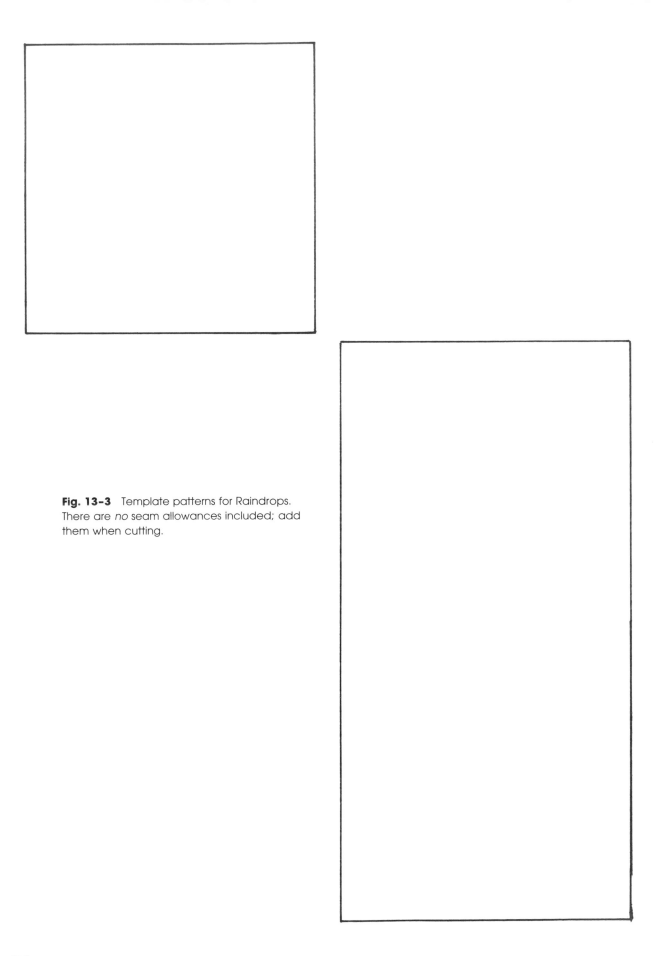

Fig. 13-3 Template patterns for Raindrops. There are *no* seam allowances included; add them when cutting.

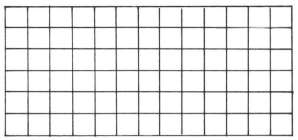

3=inch squares for projected background

background with planned floral design

Fig. 13-4 Working quilt layout for a 3-inch-square background. Photocopy the designs for color experimentation.

you move or replace it? The advantage of using this method is that patches can be moved so easily.

Hint: More 3-inch patches will be required for designing than needed for the finished quilt. Some colors/prints will work, others will not. It is impossible to really tell what works and what doesn't until the total background is pinned up and you stand back to see the total effect. Review Chapter 2: Fabrics, Colors, Kinds, Combinations.

9. Piece the background before cutting the applique patches, but read Working With Color in this chapter before making any fabric selections. The design looks different with the seam allowances taking up visual space. Uncut, each patch is 3½ inches square. You'll be surprised how much tighter and more clear the background colors look when pieced together.

10. Cut out the floral shapes (Figs. 13–7a to d) and pin onto the background. Does the design fade into the background or is it bold enough to be seen? If you are pleased, applique the design, assemble with batting and backing, and quilt. I planned to stitch-in-the-ditch (into the seam lines) and outline quilt the floral design. Bind and hang.

The Assembly Steps

Note: Do not piece or applique until you read to the end of this chapter.

1. Piece the background by sewing strips of six squares together, then joining the strips into the entire background. Press.

2. Decide on circle color and placement (see below, Working with Color). Draw around each template onto the right side of the background to place a fine-line circle in each desired location.

3. Applique to the line as in Chapter 7: Curves (Concave and Convex). When one circle covers another, applique the farthest circle first, then draw the top circle's applique line over the completed circle.

WHAT TO DO WHEN DESIGN IDEAS DON'T WORK

The small colored design discussed above (see Color Section Fig. 14). is not the same as the completed wall hanging in color section Fig. 15. What went wrong and why did I change the applique? Listed below are a number of problems that developed because of background color placement, that were not apparent until the applique design was placed.

The Trouble
Compare the color photos of the colored design and the finished piece. Notice how the colors change more gradually in the colored sample and the entire background has a lighter tone, while the finished wall hanging blends more rapidly from light to dark and is darker overall.

I tried shades of green, and teal for the leaves and a bold yellow for the flowers, but they blended into the background and visually disappeared. Next, I tried reds. While the colors were more apparent than the greens, the overall effect was a mishmash of color.

The Question
Should I start over again with lighter background colors or try to salvage it? Time and stubbornness made me want to make the pieced background work, but what should I do?

The Answer
Save the floral design (See Fig. 13–4, bottom) for use on a lighter background. Develop a new applique design for the completed background.

The Solution

The completed background was pinned onto the Styrofoam board for several days. I studied it in varying lights and also moved it from a horizontal to vertical position. My key thought was to keep the applique design *simple*.

I kept visualizing colored bubbles superimposed on the squares. Actually, I remembered yellow pine pollen highlighted by a shaft of sunlight, floating down from our fir trees in the spring. I knew a straight-edged design would not work on top of all the pieced lines and that a circular pattern would pop out from the background. With the background on the vertical, the light source now came from the top right. The "pollen" would cascade from the lightest light down and across the background to the darkest dark.

I now realized that this design was what I had wanted all along: an exercise in color placement. Deceptively simple looking, but in reality a challenge to make it work properly.

WORKING WITH COLOR

The comments below are to help you understand how to work with a variety of fabric colors/prints. I cannot tell you where to put a certain pink color or green print. This is the time for you to experiment with *your* fabrics and develop your own sense of color placement. It takes time and persistence, but the results are worth the effort.

Squares and Rectangles

Study the finished wall hanging in Color Section Fig. 15 to see what was done. Some background squares of the same fabric are next to each other. Some have been cut double into a 3 by 6 inch rectangle. Some colors are in an "L" shape and there are areas where two or three prints are together.

The rectangles were placed to break up the small squares and give the eye a rest, or to carry the eye to another spot on the background. There should not be too many rectangles, just five or seven to give interest and you might need to place them in a different spot than I did.

Chose a color that is not what you would generally put with your selected colors. Is it too bold? Or does it give interest and carry the eye throughout the design. Oranges and purples were mixed into the example to give some punch.

Circles

Once the background is completed (Fig. 13–5), the circle colors and sizes should be selected. The various

Fig. 13-5 Forest Spheres quilt layout. Notice the blocks that are rectangles rather than squares.

templates in Fig. 13–6 are the sizes used in the wall hanging. Make the circle templates and then begin cutting fabric circles.

Strong, dark reds were used rather than the dark greens in the background. Different prints in orange, green, and purple were also added. I experimented with circle sizes, limiting the use of too many small or large ones.

Begin placing darker colors in the lightest areas of the background and as you progress into to the darker, lower areas, increase the size and lighten the colors. The largest circles should only be placed in the lowest area and their color should not contrast too strongly, otherwise, the bottom of the wall hanging will draw and hold the eye.

MOVING THE VIEWER'S EYE THROUGH THE DESIGN

Study the finished wall hanging in color section Fig. 15 to understand what happens when viewing it. The viewer sees the lightest (top right) part of the background first, then locks on the small red circle and

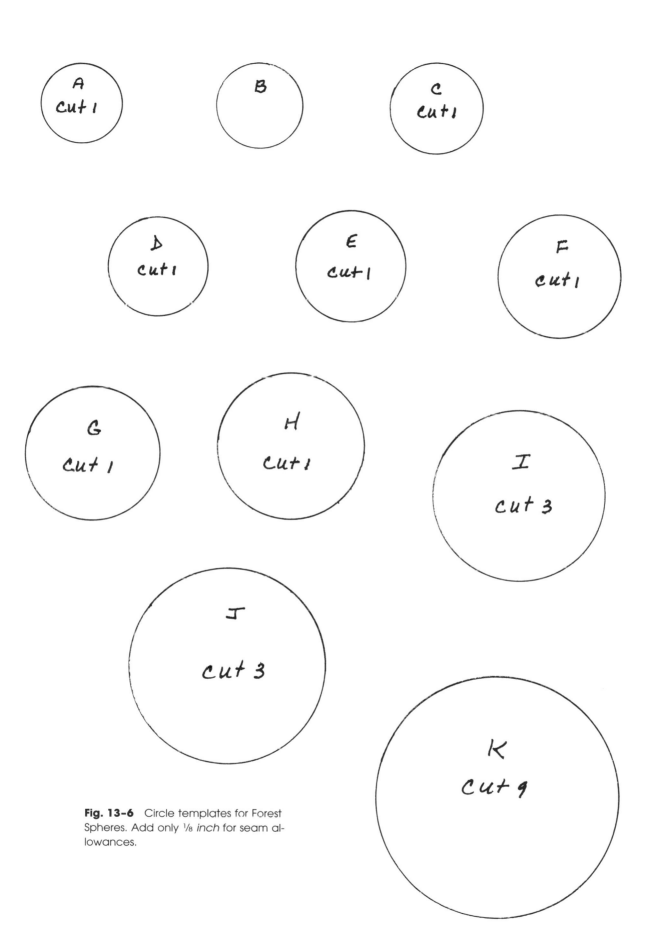

Fig. 13-6 Circle templates for Forest Spheres. Add only ⅛ *inch* for seam allowances.

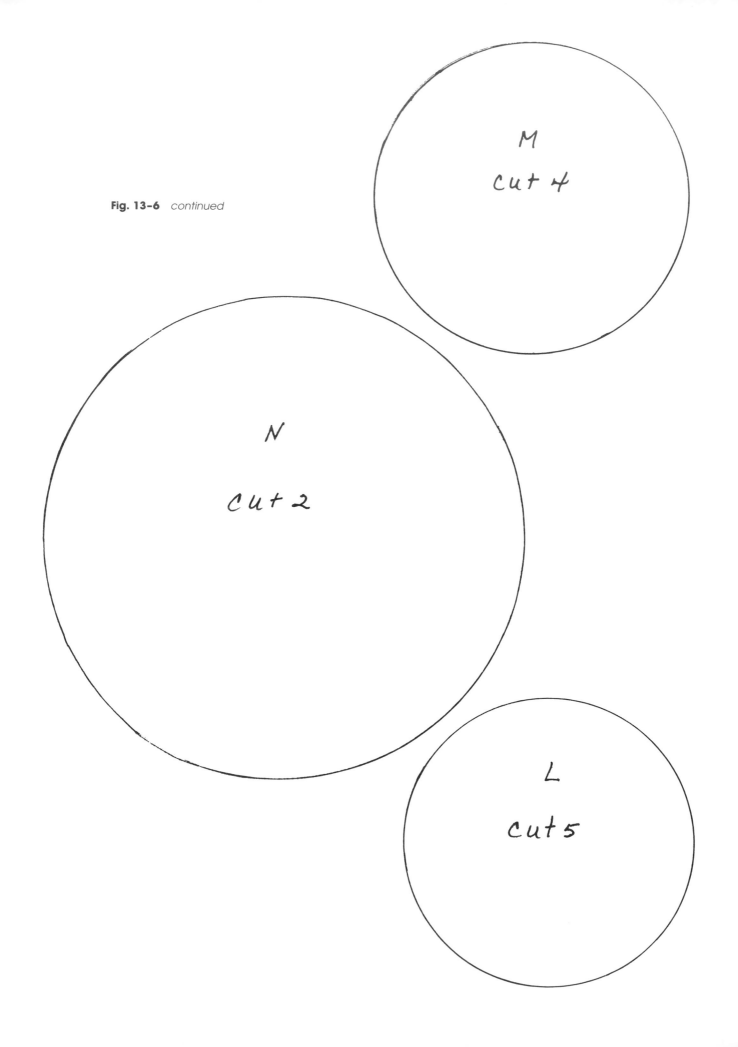

Fig. 13-6 *continued*

M
cut 4

N
cut 2

L
cut 5

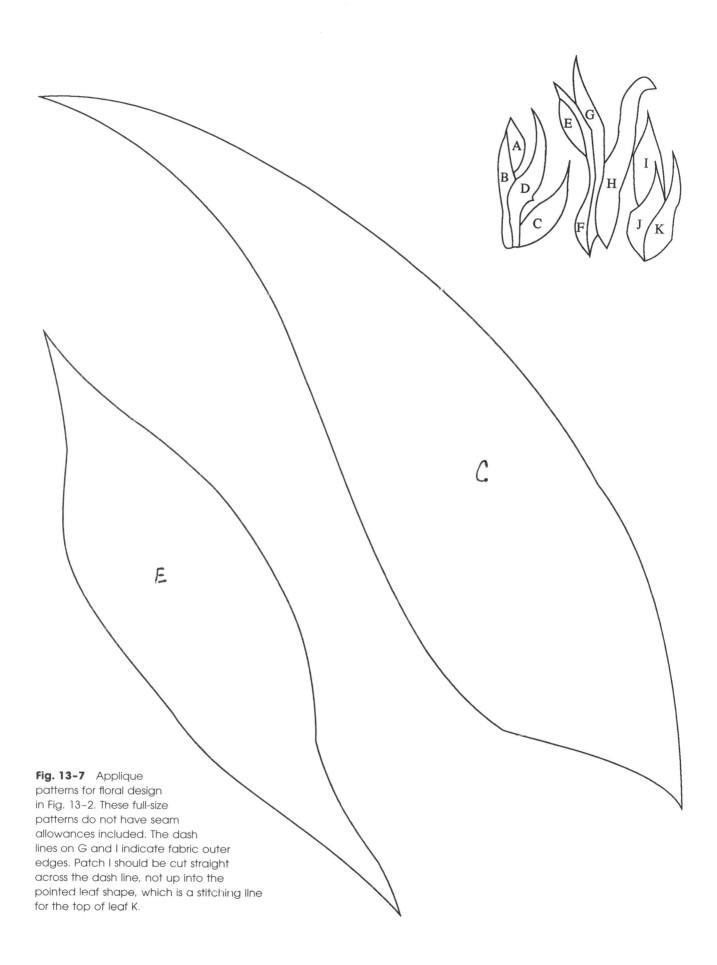

Fig. 13-7 Applique patterns for floral design in Fig. 13-2. These full-size patterns do not have seam allowances included. The dash lines on G and I indicate fabric outer edges. Patch I should be cut straight across the dash line, not up into the pointed leaf shape, which is a stitching line for the top of leaf K.

Fig. 13-7 continued

Fig. 13-7 *continued*

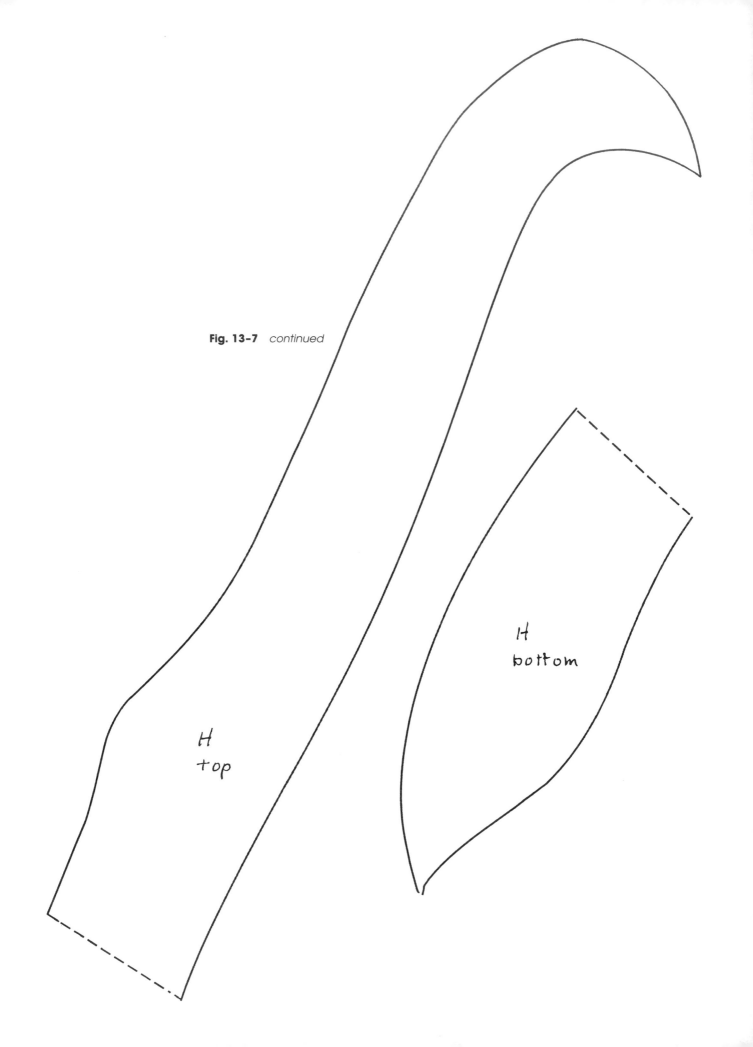

Fig. 13-7 *continued*

H
top

H
bottom

Fig. 13-7 *continued*

Fig. 13-7 *continued*

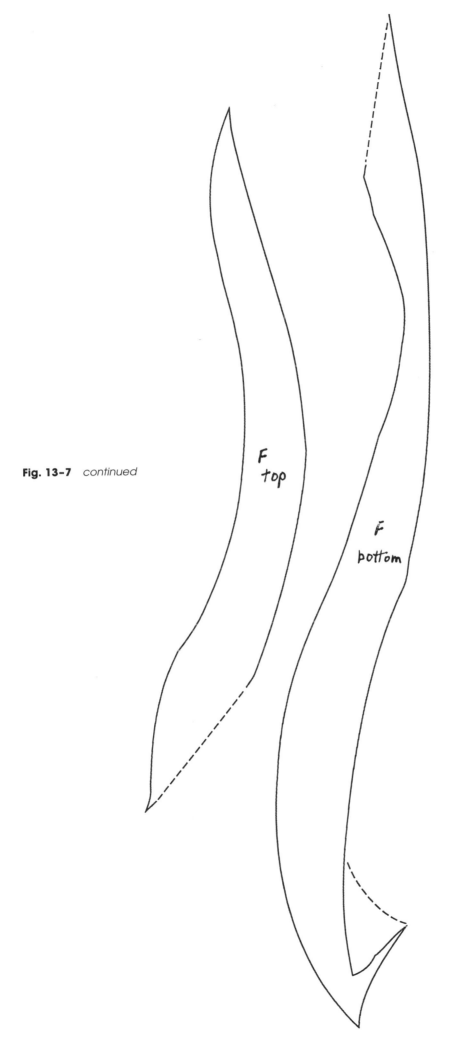

Fig. 13-7 *continued*

travels down and through the design, catching dark shapes on light squares, then light shapes on dark areas, until reaching the bottom of the wall hanging where there is a light orange circle (bottom left). The square that is second row from the bottom, second in from the right, is the same fabric as that orange circle. Unknowingly, the viewer's eye travels from the orange circle to the orange square which is overlaid with a stronger orange, set over a medium green. The eye then travels up the three yellows on the edge of the hanging, back into the design.

This deliberate placement of color and shape to carry a viewer's eye throughout the design is common to all artists. Painters use the same technique to give interest and movement to their paintings. As quilters we work with color and prints, but the technique has nothing to do with color. While it is enhanced by the element of color, variations of black and white can create this movement.

Your challenge is to learn how to use darks and lights, bold colors and muted, prints and solids, to create a harmonious design that keeps the eye circling within the quilt. The alternative is to have a design so weighted with color and shape in one area that the eye holds in one spot, ruining the flow and grace of the design.

DESIGNING WITH A COMPUTER

Quilters are putting pencil and paper aside and using computers to design quilts. The ability to instantly lay in color and pattern, shift blocks around, get accurate patterns without guesswork and create mirror images with a few keystrokes are some of the advantages of working with a computer.

It's possible to utilize a generic drawing program to create quilt designs but, to reduce frustration, look for a software package designed *specifically* for quiltmakers. These programs offer quilt basics that other drawing programs don't have, such as a library of block and border designs and multitudes of prints and colors to sample until your design approximates your fabric or vice versa.

Be aware that drawing programs require "high end" equipment, ones with more power, hard drive capacity and a color monitor.

Before purchasing any software, find out if the program will work with your computer setup. One program I've used and recommend is The Electric Quilt, from The Electric Quilt Company; Dean Neumann, Penny McMorris; 1039 Melrose St., Bowling Green, OH 43402.) Get the following information from the software manufacturer, other quiltmakers or quilt store owners:

1. Is the instruction manual written in clear, basic language?

2. Is there follow-up support from the software manufacturer?

3. Does the program do what you want it to do? Maybe you don't *know* what you want, so make sure it can do more than you think you'll need. Once proficient with computer designing, the possibilities are endless. It's conceivable to get so involved at the computer that you spend more hours designing and fewer hours actually making quilts.

4. Is the program *easy* to use? Easy is the operative word. A computer whiz will think any software program is simple. Ask that question of someone on your level of computer experience.

5. Ask other quiltmakers what program(s) they use, and why. If one program doesn't work for you, don't give up. Try another.

Once women pieced and quilted by candlelight. Today quilters work on full-color monitors. The initial methods may differ, but a quilt's beauty still touches the soul, fills the maker with pride and is a testament to its creator's skill.

Good luck. Technique is behind you. The challenge and fun begin.

Recommended Reading

The following list of quilting books was chosen to enhance or expand upon the techniques in this book. While not all the information might apply to quilt-as-you-go, each book has portions that do. Inclusion does not indicate accuracy of patterns.

The International Standard Book Number (ISBN) following each listing is a classification system for books. Its use will expedite bookstore and library ordering.

Books

Burns, Eleanor. *Irish Chain In A Day,* Quilt in a Day Publication, San Marcos, CA ISBN 0-922705-06-2

Doak, Carol. *Quiltmaker's Guide: Basics & Beyond,* American Quilter's Society, Paducah, KY ISBN 0-89145-977-4

Hanson, Joan. *Calendar Quilts,* That Patchwork Place, Bothell, WA ISBN 0-943574-77-3

Lasher, Marsha. *Scrap Quilt, Strips & Spider Webs,* Quilt in a Day Publication, San Marcos, CA ISBN 0-922705-26-7

Leman, Bonnie, and Louise Townsend. *How to Make a Quilt, 25 Easy Lessons,* MOM Publishing Company, Wheatridge, CO ISBN 0-9602970-4-9

Leone, Diana. *Fine Hand Quilting,* Leone Publications, Mountain View, CA ISBN 0-942786-48-3

Malone, Maggie. *120 Patterns for Traditional Patchwork Quilts,* Sterling Publishing Company, New York. ISBN 0-8069-7716-7

McCloskey, Marsha. *On to Square Two,* That Patchwork Place, Bothell, WA ISBN 0-943-574-97-8

McClun, Diana, and Laura Nownes. *Quilts Galore!* Quilt Digest Press, San Francisco, CA ISBN 0-912337-21-2

McCoy, Patsy R. *Amazing Mosaic Patchwork,* Kaye Wood Publishing Company, West Branch, MI ISBN 0-944588-23-9

Miller, Margaret J. *Strips That Sizzle,* That Patchwork Place, Bothell, WA ISBN 1-56477-009-5

Mumm, Debra J. *Quick Country Quilting,* Rodale Press, Emmaus, PA ISBN 0-87857-984-2

Palmer, Carolann M. *Nifty Ninepatches,* That Patchwork Place, Bothell, WA ISBN 0-943574-95-1

Poster, Donna. *The Quilter's Guide to Rotary Cutting,* Chilton Book Company, Radnor, PA ISBN 0-8019-8130-1

Remme, Camille. *Modular Magic: Module Designs for Unique Quilts,* ME Publications, Santa Monica, CA

Wolfrom, Joen. *Landscapes & Illusions,* C&T Publishing, Lafayette, CA, 1990. ISBN 0-914881-32-9

Wolfrom, Joen. *The Magical Effects of Color,* C&T Publishing, Lafayette, CA, 1992. ISBN 0-914881-53-1

Magazines

Quilter's Newsletter Magazine. Box 394, Wheat Ridge, CO 80034-0394

Quiltmaker. Box 58360, Boulder, CO 80322-8360

Quilt World. P.O. Box 11302, Des Moines, IA

Quilting International. Box 460, Mt. Morris, IL 61054

Lady's Circle Patchwork Quilts. Box 516, Mt. Morris, IL 61054

Threads. The Taunton Press, Inc., P.O. Box 5506, Newton, CT 06470-5506

Index